Morality and

*The Hoover Institution
gratefully acknowledges
the support of*

JOANNE AND JOHAN BLOKKER

on this project.

PHILOSOPHIC REFLECTIONS ON A FREE SOCIETY

Morality and Work

Edited by
Tibor R. Machan

HOOVER INSTITUTION PRESS

Stanford University   Stanford, California

www.hoover.org

Hoover Institution Press Publication No. 477
Copyright © 2000 by the Board of Trustees of the
Leland Stanford Junior University

First printing, 2000
06 05 04 03 02 01 00   9 8 7 6 5 4 3 2 1

Manufactured in the United States of America

The paper used in this publication meets the minimum requirements
of American National Standard for Information Sciences—Permanence
of Paper for Printed Library Materials, ANSI Z39.48-1984. ♾

Library of Congress Cataloging-in-Publication Data
Morality and work / edited by Tibor R. Machan.
    p.   cm.
Includes bibliographical references and index.
ISBN 0-8179-9852-7 (alk. paper)
    1. Work—Moral and ethical aspects. I. Machan, Tibor R.
HD4905 .M69 2000
174′.4—dc21   00-021785

CONTENTS

ACKNOWLEDGMENTS

I WISH to express my gratitude to the Hoover Institution on War, Revolution and Peace, and its director, John Raisian, for generously supporting the publication of this work. Heartfelt thanks also go to Joanne and Johan Blokker for their generous support of my scholarly projects at the Hoover Institution. I also wish to thank the contributing authors for their cooperation, patience, and conscientiousness throughout the entire publishing process. Last, but not least, I wish to thank Pat Baker, Ann Wood, and Marshall Blanchard of the Hoover Institution Press for their extensive and very helpful assistance with the completion of this volume.

CONTRIBUTORS

TIBOR R. MACHAN is Freedom Communications, Inc., Professor at the Leatherby Center for Entrepreneurship and Business Ethics, at the Argyros School of Business and Economics, Chapman University and Research Fellow at the Hoover Institution.

JAMES CHESHER is Professor of Philosophy at Santa Barbara City College. He co-authored *The Business of Commerce, Examining an Honorable Profession* for the Hoover Institution Press (1999).

PAUL HEYNE taught economics at the University of Washington and was author of the widely used text, *The Economic Way of Thinking*, which is now in its 9th edition (Prentice-Hall, 1999). He died in April 2000.

DWIGHT R. LEE is Professor of Economics at the University of Georgia. He wrote *Next Environmental Battleground: Indoor Air* (National Center for Policy Analysis, 1992) and co-authored *Failure and Progress: The Bright Side of the Dismal Science* (Cato Institute, 1993).

RICHARD B. MCKENZIE is the Walter B. Gerken Professor of Enterprise and Society in the Graduate School of Management at the University of California, Irvine. He wrote *Managing Through Incentives* (1998) and *Getting Rich in America* (1999), both written with Dwight Lee.

THE REVEREND ROBERT SIRICO is the President of the Acton Institute and a frequent contributor to the *Wall Street Journal* and other publications. He wrote the book *Moral Basis for Liberty* (Coronet Books, 1994).

GREGORY M. A. GRONBACHER, PH.D., is director of the Center for Economic Personalism at the Acton Institute for the Study of Religion and Liberty in Grand Rapids, Michigan.

Morality and Work

Tibor R. Machan

THIS BOOK CONCERNS ethical issues related to work. I say "work" instead of "labor" because as widely used, the concept of labor suggests that some of what we do is laboring, some of it another thing entirely, as we produce the goods and services that people want and are willing to pay for. Labor has this odor of discomfort about it, as if all of it had to be a chore. And it also carries with it the connotation that it involves mainly, if not exclusively, physical activity.

"Work," in turn, is broader in its meaning. Most of us work, whether or not what we work at is satisfying. Ideally, some would argue, we should try to find something to work at that is pleasant, even personally fulfilling.

An individualist view of human nature would suggest that there could be great varieties of pleasant, fulfilling work and some will find rewarding what others detest doing. This supports a benign view of the division of labor. It is not only because that division furthers overall efficiency and prosperity, but also because human nature is best accommodated if there are many different kinds of work to be done by which we can prosper. The challenge is to find the line of work that suits oneself and turn it into a profitable task.

Collectivists conceptions of work, in contrast, have a "one size fits all" model and look for the day when everyone can do what it is best suited for human beings as such to do. Marx thought, for example, that everyone would flourish from being an intellectual (in communist society), following, with significant detours, the ideas of Aristotle who also believed that the truly happy life must be focused on theoretical endeavors.

The individualist approach to this subject seems much closer to being right than what the collectivists offer. The very fact that we all have different histories—consisting of physical, cultural, psychological, and moral differences—suggests that it is a mistake to think that there is one kind of work that is best for us all. In addition, each of us has a decisive hand in the direction of our lives. We take all the factors that are given and consciously guide to what end they will be utilized, whether we will change some, abandon a few, and develop yet others to some advantage.

Still, it is true enough that in some matters we are all alike, in our basic humanity, which also includes being individuals who need to be true to who they are. And there is where ethics come into full view.

It is within the field of ethics that the question arises of, "How should I (a human being) act?" or, "By what standards should I conduct myself?" The reason this occurs for us is that unlike other animals, human beings lack a full range of instincts to prompt their suitable, life-sustaining behavior. In the place of instincts, human beings seem to have the capacity to initiate mental focus (on the world) and then select what is or is not important to do. Ethical theorizing—or moral philosophy—devotes itself to figuring out what is important, most generally, so our selections could be right.

When it comes to the sphere of applied ethics—a branch of ethics focusing on distinct areas of human concern—there is little consensus as to what ethical theory is right. But in the case of the ethics of commerce, of which labor or work is a subdivision, at least this much can be said: The virtue of prudence, the first of the cardinal virtues, underpins this sphere of human conduct. That is to say, we ought to make sure, among other things, that we take care of our needs and wants and those of our loved ones, diligently and carefully.

In the communities in which we live, this implies that, among other things, we ought to produce and trade competently. One of the benefits we can trade is our work capacity. We have skills, knowledge, and time, and, in return for these, we can often obtain goods and services from others, one's we want more than keeping what we already have.

To fail to trade well when we have needs and wants to fulfill is neglectful, reckless, even imprudent. Diligence, industry, frugality, thrift, enterprise, and other more specific virtues characterize prudence as it is applied to commerce.

In any case, the task we have in this volume is to spell out some of the special ethical dimensions of work. Before our contributors embark on the details of this task, however, I wish to discuss labor, as it is generally viewed, namely, as making a living through hardship.

Most economists have seen labor as a cost: we would avoid it if we could. Leisure, in contrast, is a benefit. In addition, labor has for centuries been contrasted with management, the arm of capitalists who, by some accounts, have hardly anything to contribute to productivity. Must this be so? Couldn't labor and management be merged, conceptually and actually?

First, it seems there is no reason to continue with the unfortunately entrenched dichotomy between labor and management. This is more an artificial product of law, which itself derives from pre-capitalist times when classes were fixed by misconceived political and social philosophies, institutions, and practices. It seems much more sensible, as hinted before, to think of work as the category that encompasses what labor and management artificially divide.

As far as the law is concerned, then, there should be no Department of Labor at all, no National Right to Work legislation, no labor unions and such. Instead there could well be varieties of labor corporations, analogous to professional partnerships. Thus, machinists, autoworkers, or postal workers, instead of unionizing, might well form a professional company that may be retained for various jobs by various people or other companies. This is akin to how construction companies function, only here the workers would be partners of the firm.

Second, the idea of wage—or salary—labor raises the specter of some morally odious results, such as unfair exploitation and the belief in job security. In a free market place no job security can exist because customers cannot be conscripted. Only governments can offer job security—including tenure—as a matter of course because they obtain income via taxation, although even this can come to a halt under certain circumstances.

Third, the polarization between labor and management is an impediment to productivity. Strikes bring production to a standstill for long periods of time, and they depend for their existence on this obsolete polarization. In partnerships there are no strikes, only occasional negotiations. Subcontracting with different firms is also largely cooperative, even if there remain possible internal disagreements, as there are in many organizations. Such disputes occur simply because of our tendency to pitch our own individual or partisan visions of how a firm should be structured and how the organization as a whole should behave. There need, and should, be no entrenched (class) conflicts in markets.

The basic ethics of any profession are concerned solely with how to further the lawful aims for which the profession exists. Of course, "lawfulness" can sometimes pose a problem, since the law may itself embody sources of conflict, as is the case with the legally entrenched polarization between labor and management that I just mentioned and that will be treated by some of the contributors to this volume.

For example, if a federal agency such as the Food and Drug Administration sets policies that violate basic property or other individual rights, so that a drug lag is created between different markets—

those, say, in Canada and the USA—professional ethics will be distorted. The aim to serve consumers with effective, if at times risky, goods and services would require companies to bring to market what the law bans or severely regulates. (Remedy for harmful conduct would be sought via civil law and would not violate the prohibition against prior restraint.)

Subsidies to various firms establish entrenched unfairness that companies then will be tempted to circumvent so as to fulfill their professional duty to help their owners' prosperity. Licensing can favor vested interests—some professions gaining, others failing to gain lawfulness (e.g., licensed psychologists versus unorthodox ones that are excluded from the field of competition).

Morality requires freedom. One cannot do the right thing without freedom from interference. Only when rights violations are involved are legal bans justified.

Failing to pay "a fair wage," however, isn't a violation of rights, even if there could be, on special occasions, certain moral objections raised involving fairness. Once the state imposes a minimum wage, subsidies, or price support measures, a vital condition for doing the right thing, namely freedom of choice on the part of all traders, is violated. What is left is legal maneuvering that often focuses not on what is right, but on what enables a company to gain legally supported breaks in increasing the market for their goods and services. In much of the labor market there are innumerable such violations. Although some efforts at doing the right thing may still be made, the distortion will tend to demoralize the labor market. (For more on this, see Tibor R. Machan, ed., *Business Ethics in the Global Market* [Hoover Press, 1999].)

Some of these matters will be discussed extensively in this book; others will be touched upon only briefly, mainly so as to raise the matter for readers who might then consider ways of dealing with them. Our aim here is to confront several of the basic issues of the morality of the labor market, including offering some alternatives to conventional ways of understanding that market.

CHAPTER ONE

The Ethics of Employment

James Chesher

MORAL ISSUES arising out of, and relevant to, employment come from a more general and more fundamental background of moral concerns: on the one hand, theoretical questions about the nature of morality, and, on the other, moral questions about the actual practice and professional ethics of the activity of commerce, of which employment is a part. A few words about each is in order, beginning with commerce.

Commerce shares this interesting feature with life: Success is measured, in part, by longevity, survival, and continued existence. This is because in life, as well as in commerce, serious failures typically result in disaster, often in death. In both life and commerce, there is a general requirement to be cautious, intelligent, prepared—in short, prudent. The basic goal of individuals engaging in commerce is economic flourishing; the basic goal of individuals in living their lives is a more general kind of flourishing known as happiness.

Now, when it comes to realizing economic flourishing, there are all manner of things to know, rules to follow, considerations to weigh. Some of these are of a strictly commercial nature, having to do with, for example, questions of capital investment, marketing, accounting, etc.; some are of a strictly legal nature, involving such things as attention to government regulations, licensing, tax payments; others are of a more general social nature, having to do with, for instance, maintaining the reputation and integrity of one's business. So, too, are there many dimensions to successfully living a life.

Clearly, for those many people who engage in commerce professionally, their being in business is an integral part of their living a life. Put another way, their goal of happiness, which they share with all other human beings, is realized, in part, by the extent to which they achieve their goal of commercial success. It is no secret that commercial success, success at making a living, is not identical with success at living a life. Indeed, it is quite possible that, in the pursuit of fortune, one risks, abandons, or forfeits one's claim to success at living. This means that, in both commerce and in living, one can pursue one's goals poorly, moderately well, or admirably, and this fact gives rise to morality. Since commerce arises from the profession of business, and given that the activity of business produces moral questions and problems, business ethics must be seen as a branch of professional ethics, growing out of human commerce, and deserving of serious consideration.

With this in mind, namely, that moral questions within employment come from the more general human activity of commerce, and that such questions arise against the more general and fundamental theoretical area of moral philosophy, we can now turn specifically to an exploration of the ethics of employment.

EMPLOYMENT ETHICS

It is hardly possible in contemporary American society to talk about moral issues that arise in the workplace and in the employment relationship, apart from legal considerations. Discussion about workers' rights, hourly wage, safety on the job, overtime pay, benefits, hiring and termination practices, and so on, inevitably involves reference to various state and federal regulations, laws, and guidelines. Such is the pervasiveness of government, that it has become not only the rather visible hand that directs the various aspects of employment, but shapes, as well, the way we think and talk about it. Consider the questions: "What is a fair wage?" "How many hours a day or a week ought a person be expected to work?" "Who is responsible for injuries to a worker on the job?" "Is it right for an employer to hire whomever he/she wishes despite qualifications?" "What may an employer expect of an employee in terms of effort, honesty, loyalty to the company, etc?" "What may an employee expect from an employer in terms of protection from workplace hazards, job security, additional pay for especially productive work, freedom from unwanted or disrespectful treatment such as sexual harassment, acts of prejudice, bias, exploitation, and the like?" These, and many others related to them, are legitimate moral questions, well worth exploring, but the purely moral dimension of these questions has given way to legal answers brought about, at least in some measure, by political, i.e., coercive, as opposed to social or moral, pressures.

And so, a "fair" minimum wage is established by Congress; OSHA oversees worker health and safety. For many workers, hourly employment that exceeds forty hours per week, or eight hours a day, or some such number, must be paid a premium; workers must be given at least one ten-minute break for every four continuous hours of work (or some such formula); there is an extended family leave provision guaranteed by federal law; and so on. The laws, rules, and regulations overseen and enforced by the federal Department of Labor cover every conceivable aspect of employment and number into the thousands.[1] In addition, there are countless state laws and regulations

1. For a "Mission Statement" and legislation data relevant to the U.S. Department of Labor, see the following Web site: www.dol.gov/dol/public/aboutdol/main.htm.

that impact on, if not directly govern, aspects of employment. It is fair to observe that these many laws and regulations are designed to protect the worker from abuse and neglect by employers, on the assumption that workers generally do not have sufficient power to persuade employers to provide them with the desirable wages, benefits, and conditions that these laws and regulations mandate under threat of force through penalties and other deterrents.[2] In other words, the perceived justification for these laws and regulations are the social benefits of the increased well-being of workers—that is, an overall reduction of human suffering that, the reasoning goes, would have existed but for these laws. Thus, a moral principle (in this case, utility, increased happiness) serves as rationale for the legal mandates. Now, a historical case for the necessity of state involvement in the workplace can certainly be made, citing, for example, the abysmal working conditions of early industrialization. That such conditions existed are beyond dispute, though whether state, and thus coercive, solutions were (and presently are) the best moral response is surely debatable.[3]

Putting this aside, and granting that suffering is in fact reduced by government regulation and statutes, and granting further that laws generally serve to prevent suffering, it still does not follow from these facts alone that such regulations and laws are morally justified. For example, a law prohibiting the eating of junk food or requiring daily exercise, if strictly enforced, would likely reduce human suffering but would hardly be justified and would certainly be unwelcome even

---

2. Other factors may also contribute to the existence of such laws, such as promises of benefits to large blocks of voters in exchange for votes. What may be questionable, both morally and economically (e.g., a mandated minimum wage), becomes the expected, the valued, the norm of decency, etc., once it gets legal sanction and enjoys the respectability of having come into being through the democratic process.

3. See J. E. Chesher, "Business: Myth and Morality," in *Business Ethics & Common Sense*, ed. Robert W. McGee (Westport, Conn.: Quorum Books, 1992), pp. 45–65.

by many of those who exercise and have healthful diets. It is arguable, if not widely and rightly understood, that there are limits to the proper intervention of law and that some matters ought to remain private and left up to the discretion of the individual.[4] Where the lines are drawn is, of course, a matter of dispute, as evidenced by major political differences between, say, liberals, conservatives, and libertarians with respect to the extent to which government ought to direct the affairs of its citizens. As a matter of observable fact, there is hardly a dimension of human life, hardly a possible human relationship, that escapes the directing force of law and regulation. This means that contemporary life is profoundly shaped by the law, that individual deliberation, choice, initiative, and discretion are largely determined by government and are thus essentially political, rather than moral, in quality. To the extent that this is so, it could be argued that the moral space within which decisions are made is quite small, with little room for genuine moral struggle, discovery, and the expression, even growth, of character that such struggle makes possible.

None of this is meant as an appeal to reconsider labor laws—though no doubt a good many of the laws and regulations (e.g., minimum wage laws) could be shown to produce more suffering and result in greater overall economic loss and injustice than their proponents evidently realize.[5] Rather, the point is that, contrary to ap-

---

4. An irony of contemporary politics is that the very moral principle that is often appealed to for justification of government spending and the limitations on freedom created by regulations, namely, utilitarianism, was given sharp limits ignored in wholesale fashion by the very people who invoke action in the name of the greater good. John Stuart Mill, in his famous essay "The Tyranny of the Majority," argues that there are moral limits to what can be mandated. In other words, Mill himself argued that majority rule, or majority benefit, does not in itself justify action that brings it about; there are some actions that even the majority may not rightfully impose. Examples abound.

5. It is fair to say that the overwhelming body of economic research generally supports the view that government intervention in a market economy (by means of regulation, wage and price control, subsidies, etc.), often creates greater problems than the intervention was intended to solve or prevent. This has been shown time

pearances, the employment relationship is fundamentally and essentially moral rather than legal, social rather than political, and personal rather than institutional. The purpose of this chapter is to revisit employment, to explore the employer-employee relationship from a moral perspective, and to determine which principles ought to guide the employer-employee relationship and employer-employee conduct, as well as to settle conflicts that arise in the workplace. Such principles should enlighten us as to the limits and proper application of laws governing employment. In short, I wish to address the question, "What are the ethics of employment?"

It may be helpful to begin by observing that morality is possible (and necessary) because human beings are capable of suffering harm and being benefited by actions that result from human choices. In general, where there is no harm, there can hardly be a wrong, but not every harm constitutes a wrong. Someone surely can be harmed accidentally, or by an act of nature, without thereby having been wronged. What counts as a wrong depends upon the discovery of certain standards of evaluation that apply to human conduct. These simple and fundamental facts, that choice, harm, and standards are central to morality, make living a human life an inherently and continuously unfolding, moral process. Further, that human beings can be harmed in multiple ways and that human choices are often made in variously complex situations accounts, in part, for the disagreements that often arise as to what ought to be done. Moral deliberation, guided by moral principles, is the appropriate method of resolving such conflicts. Even in those many cases when conflict resolution turns on appeal to laws or regulations, the ultimate force of such statutes itself derives from a moral principle. In other words, a just

---

and again with say, minimum wage laws. For continuous examination of the often hidden costs and socioeconomic dislocations caused by government intervention, as well as for proposed alternatives consistent with political liberty and free markets, see *Reason* magazine, which for over thirty years has defended free markets and free minds.

resolution must be more than simply a legal one, if it is to be fully satisfactory.

Since there is also occasional disagreement about the standards and the principles of deliberation, moral philosophy is necessary as a theoretical backdrop to first-order moral discourse. Now, given such disagreements, it would seem illogical to embark upon a study of the ethics of employment without first settling the theoretical disputes. After all, would there not be different perspectives, different principles and standards from which to approach the question?

As a matter of practical necessity, the resolution of actual moral problems (now commonly referred to as "applied ethics" when approached in a disciplined way and distinct from theoretical ethics and metaethics) cannot and need not await the resolution of theoretical disputes, any more than practical questions about how much weight a bridge can support or whether one can mix different cleaning solutions together can and must await resolution of disagreements in theoretical physics and chemistry. Were we required to settle theory prior to practice, little would get accomplished in actual life. This presents an apparent paradox: If, as stated earlier, moral problems are appropriately settled by reference to standards and principles, and if standards and principles are themselves in dispute at the theoretical level, how can moral problems be settled at all until the theoretical questions are answered?

First, theory is neither factually nor logically prior to practice. Even in the sciences our experience of the world precedes our explanations of those experiences. We engage in theoretical study in order to offer intellectually compelling accounts of our experiences. Put broadly and simply, the best theoretical account is that which explains our experiences most fully, comprehensively, and most free of internal inconsistency as well as free of conflict with our understanding of the rest of our experiences. The idea is that a careful study of the world will reveal principles in terms of natural laws, predictively reliable significant correlations, or some other regularities indicative of the nature and order of phenomena. These principles, then, can serve as guides or standards for additional, yet unexplained, phenomena, or, in the matter of human personal, social, and political life, as guides to conduct. Thus, it is a mistake to think of theory as preceding practice, and of practice as being dependent on the completion of theoretical investigation.

Second, that there is theoretical dispute within moral philosophy does not make applied ethics any less possible than do disagreements in theoretical physics make problem solving in, say, auto mechanics impossible. In fact, there is sufficient agreement among moral philosophers and people generally, concerning the vices and virtues and the ends of moral conduct, to provide guidance in practical life.

Third, that theoretical differences will likely sometimes yield incompatible solutions in applied ethics is a good reason to focus on actual moral problems, for doing so can bring to the surface theoretical assumptions that may require responding to challenge. The most difficult cases are the ones most likely to put our principles to the test, and competing principles will force a call for justifications. So, let us begin.

CLEARING THE WAY

Discussion of employment ethics should begin with an account of the nature of employment and of the relationship between employer and employee. At once we come upon a possible obstacle, as the roles of employee and employer are subject to widespread cultural mythology that tends to conceive of the relationship as inherently adversarial and unfair, with one side, employer, enjoying all of the advantages that accrue to a favorable differential of power. And so the employee, the worker (as though the employer does no work!), is considered something of a servant, slave, or property of the employer, who is pictured (quite unabashedly, in the popular entertainment media) as the master, the boss, who rules over all, and whose word is law. The employee is seen as the often helpless, overworked, underpaid victim of the often tyrannical, stingy employer (from which comes the pejorative "scrooge") who reigns as master to slave or lord to serf. This picture derives much of its power and plausibility from the historical origins of labor being forced upon slaves, and of the long period of feudal serfdom, followed by the industrial revolution of the early modern era, which saw all manner of worker suffering and abuse. It is also supported by the intellectual movement of liberalism, beginning with the enlightenment, branching off into suspicion of anything less than complete egalitarianism, and culminating in the form of Marxist thought.[6]

However understandable and rooted in history and intellectual tradition, this view of the employment relationship is not adequate for our purposes. To begin with, the slave-master model, inherently immoral, can hardly serve as a model for the employment relationship. There can be no serious answer to the question, "What are the ethics of slavery?" Secondly, whatever vestiges of slave, feudal, and early industrial abuses exist in contemporary society are just that— vestiges, residual features of an earlier time, no longer applicable to present circumstances. We should be aware that the picture, which still holds many people captive as they talk about employment, is as metaphorical as our talk of the sun rising and setting, but with greater social consequence. Assuming, then, that the popular model is deficient, let us return to the question of the nature of the employment relationship. What do we see?

In contrast with the rest of the animal kingdom, human beings must work in order to live. Among the earliest of the Babylonian myths is the story of the victory of the god Marduk over his divine adversaries. From the blood of the defeated gods, so the story goes, Marduk fashioned out human beings to perform labor for him. This

6. For a discussion of the influence of Marx on the myth of worker as slave, see Chesher, pp. 59–61.

myth answered the ancient but enduring question, "Why must man labor?" Clearly, the answer, "Because Marduk wanted someone else to do the work" is hardly satisfactory, but it does point to an inescapable fact of human life, that we must work. Even today, with the assistance of technology, few people escape this fate. Given the various necessities, not to mention the amenities, of life, one must work for their procurement, either on one's own or, in some manner, in relationship with others. The principle of the division of labor, championed early on in the modern period by Adam Smith, illustrates how inefficient it generally is for individuals to attempt solitary production of whatever will satisfy all of one's needs. This was discovered in prehistoric times and developed into a full-blown, widespread practice with the advent of modern technology, industrialization, and insight into the sources of the creation of wealth.

Now, since solitary production is on the whole unsatisfactory, we have the option of working in relationship with others. This can take a variety of forms: partnerships, cooperatives of various sorts, including corporations, trade, and, of particular interest here, employment. These various relationships are all commercial, involving in one way or another the exchange of goods, services, or labor for the sake of securing, from the point of view of all participants, something valued.

Thus, commercial activity, including employment, is, from its origins to its ends, normative in character. We engage in work and enter into commercial relationships, including employment, in order to realize valued ends. Further, though necessary for human life, whether to work at all, to what extent, and in what way, is volitional, a matter of choice. Unlike animals, who are driven by nature to do what they do, human beings recognize that they have a choice even in whether to exert effort to do what it takes to live, to be, or not to be. This capacity to choose includes, inherently, the choice of the very standard according to which choices are to be made. Were this not so, human efforts to encourage others, to remonstrate with them, to argue, to praise and blame, would be idle ceremonies.

These two basic features of commercial life, value and choice based upon a standard, which are features of all human activities, make employment and the employment relationship fundamentally moral. That is, one enters into an employment relationship voluntarily and with the aim of benefit to oneself, by offering the other party to the relationship something, such as one's labor, skill, or talent, that the other values and sees as of benefit. Were it not voluntary, it would be slavery, and calling it "employment" would be a euphemism at best. Were there no expected value, one could hardly explain the proposed exchange. Of course, it may well be that the choices available to one side or the other are few or great, and this will likely affect the value of what is offered for exchange, as well as the terms of the exchange itself. If what one has to offer is in great supply, one ought not expect its exchange value to be as great as if the demand were much greater than the supply, and vice-versa. This is so for either side of the exchange. For example, when it comes to employment, a worker who has relatively few skills to offer will, to that extent, have fewer opportunities for employment; the employer who has relatively fewer benefits or lower wages to offer will, to that extent, attract fewer qualified workers. This explains the quite common (and commonsensical) advice that elders give to the young about getting a higher education, or, if not that, of acquiring skills that are in demand. It also explains why employers, in search of the best candidate for an opening, are (or, anyway, ought to be) willing to pay a premium wage and additional benefits.

What affects the relative worth of labor, services, wages, benefits, etc., is a complex matter well beyond the scope of this chapter. Suffice it to say that, whatever the sources affecting supply and demand, the matter of concern here remains clear: the employment relationship is entered into voluntarily, if not always eagerly, and with the understanding of mutual benefit, if not always mutually acknowledged.

In essence, then, the employment relationship is a contract, an agreement by each side to offer the other something that the other values. This establishes moral boundaries and provides a guide for the proper workings of the relationship. That is, the nature of the relationship, that it is voluntary and mutually beneficial, along with the particular details of the contract agreed to by both sides, provide the criteria by which the actual workings of the relationship are to be assessed, conflicts are resolved, changes made, and, in the end, the relationship is terminated.

In short, the ethics of employment are grounded in the model of employment as a contract between consenting, mutually self-interested adults. Clearly, this relationship can take a number of forms, and the particulars of the contract may vary widely depending upon the parties involved, the work or service to be performed, the conditions under which the relationship operates, and other factors. One party may offer to provide labor or some other service for a set fee or in exchange for something else of value. This could be as simple as one party offering to haul trash for another in exchange for, say, $50, or as complicated as one party offering another financial advice on a business venture in exchange for, say, an hourly rate on a sliding fee based on some agreed-to standard and/or a percentage of the profits of the business, a share in ownership, or some other arrangement contingent on one or another specifiable condition among many.

It is not always clear whether a commercial relationship is an employment relationship or some other commercial arrangement, since it is not always clear who has hired whom, and what counts as hiring. In one sense, a homeowner who contracts with, say, a roofer to replace his roof for a specified amount, has hired the roofer, who in turn is in the homeowner's employ. The roofer, in turn, may have workers do the actual labor in exchange for an hourly rate. Though the homeowner has hired the roofer, the roofer's workers are not thought of as employed by the homeowner, since their agreement is with the roofer and not the homeowner. Had the homeowner contracted directly with the workers, he/she could properly be said to have hired them, and the workers could then be said to have been in his employ, at least for the duration of the job.

But suppose that, in the first instance, the roofer had agreed to provide a roof not for money but in exchange for the homeowner's providing in return, say, so many meals at the homeowner's restaurant, or so many auto tune-ups from the homeowner, a mechanic. Who has hired whom? Who is in whose employ? What should be stressed here is not so much the question itself, but a feature of employment that is often overlooked, and which this question brings to surface: The nature of the employment relationship, being grounded in voluntary agreement to a mutually beneficial exchange, is essentially reciprocal, one of moral equality. That is, the question of who is in whose employ is not a morally relevant consideration. What is relevant are the terms of the agreement and the extent to which each party honors those terms. One can be employed by another in exchange for an hourly rate, for a fixed salary, for so much produced, for a commission, for a share in the profits, for an indefinite number of other various considerations, or any combination of these. In other words, employment can take many forms, and questions appropriate to one form of employment may not be appropriate to others.

Now, the paradigm conception of employment, and certainly the most common and that which figures in most discussions of the employer-employee relationship, is where one party, the employer, hires another, the employee, to work for him/her for an hourly wage, over an extended period of time, usually understood as extending into the indefinite future. It is generally pictured that the employer is a firm or a company, a private business offering products or a service to customers. (Let us leave aside public employment, which raises unique questions not relevant to our concerns, not the least of which is that the employer of a public employee is, ultimately, the tax-paying citizenry, which includes the employee! There are political factors inherent in public employment, as well as problems unique to the public sphere that would require lengthy treatment beyond the scope of this essay. Additionally, government employment necessarily involves complex legal and bureaucratic considerations, which would unnecessarily complicate our inquiry, which focuses on the moral aspect of employment. In short, not every legal obligation, right, or limitation is a moral one. However, generally, what we say about the ethics of employment should apply to public employment, though with a host of qualifications.)

Given this necessarily general understanding of who is employee and who is employer, let us now address some basic questions about the nature and moral aspects of this relationship.

THE ETHICS OF EMPLOYMENT

The employment relationship is essentially contractual, reciprocal, and entered into by both parties on equal terms. This last feature, equality, does not mean that each party is equally in need of the particular other for the benefit sought, nor does it mean that each has equal opportunity, resources, or desire to otherwise secure that which an employment agreement would bring. The facts of supply and demand bear directly on which side has the bargaining advantage, exactly as they would in any other commercial transaction. Generally speaking, the so-called employer, the one seeking to hire (being the one in need of another's labor, skill, or services), has more resources and usually more candidates to choose from, than the prospective employee, the one seeking to be hired. The latter likely has more competition from other prospective employees. In short, it is generally the case that there is a greater supply of prospective employees than of employers. This of course means that for any given employer, any particular prospective employee is less significant, less necessary for the realization of the employer's ends. Any one of many potential employees may well satisfy the employer's needs. On this matter, the employer clearly enjoys more of the power that comes from having greater opportunities. In general, to terminate an agreement with any given particular employee is less traumatic and threatening to the employer's ends than the reverse would be for the employee, whose opportunities for alternative employment may be comparatively few.

Now, these general facts are not unique to employment; they obtain in all commercial transactions to varying degrees, depending ultimately on the law of supply and demand. Further, whether supply and demand favors the employer or the employee is also variable. In some instances, for example, in certain dynamic and rapidly growing industries such as computer programming a few years back, or Web-based communication technology as of this writing, the demand for qualified prospective employees may exceed supply. It may also be the case that an employee will make more money than his/her employer. It is certainly the case that some employees, for example, certain salespersons, earn more money than a good many employers, for instance, owners of corner markets and other modest businesses. So, contrary perhaps to the popular view, simply because someone is an employee does not, of itself, guarantee that the person is at any disadvantage with respect to his/her employer. Thus, though the power differential may in general side with the employer, it does not always, which means that there is nothing in the employment relationship as such that favors either side. To repeat, each side is free to accept (or refuse) the employment terms of the other, each enters into the relationship voluntarily and self-interestedly, and each recognizes the mutually beneficial value of the agreement. Each is also free to terminate the relationship (subject to the terms of the agreement). In the end, the employer and employee enter the relationship as moral peers, equally bound to honor the terms. That is, in coming to terms, each recognizes the rights and obligations of the other to abide by the terms. They could, of course, make their agreement a legally binding contract, violation of which would put one at legal risk, but this goes beyond the moral dimension of the relationship and of our present interests.

THE TERMS

The only thing that can be said a priori about the contract or agreement that creates the employment relationship is that the terms establish the moral boundaries within which each side must act. Nothing can be determined in advance about the specifics of the agreement. Particulars are bound to vary from time to time, place to place, and from person to person. For instance, what counts as a fair and attractive wage will vary not only from industry to industry, but also from individual to individual, depending upon a host of personal, economic, and social factors. It is impossible to specify what the terms or their limits ought to be, apart from an actual context. In general, the terms agreed to will be determined by what each side has to offer and by the value of those offerings as perceived by both parties. Now, though the particulars of the terms may vary widely, there are general moral limits to what may be offered by either side as well as to what each side may accept. These limits, in turn, may vary depending upon the moral perspective, philosophy, or principle that serves as a guide. For example, what is permissible from, say, the Utilitarian perspective may not be permissible from the Kantian, or the Egoist, or the theistic perspective.

However, though these schools of thought differ in some fundamental way from each other, they are in great general agreement about many features of morality. For example, they agree about the importance of the virtues and the principle that human beings should avoid harm to innocent others whenever possible, that one ought to keep one's word, and so on. These, just mentioned themselves, imply a host of corollaries that form an interlocking web of guiding principles that are the source of everyday, commonsense morality. Much of which, not surprisingly, is consistent with the principles of the major moral theories.

When persons enter into agreements as moral equals, such as when they enter into an employment relationship, this web of principles provides the limiting conditions within which the terms of the agreement are morally acceptable and binding. Many of these principles are so entrenched in and, indeed, inherent to common social life that they rarely rise to the level of consciousness; for example, that, in general, people are expected to, and do, in fact, tell the truth and keep their word. Were this not so, we would hardly do any of such countless ordinary things as asking a total stranger for directions to the airport!

Human social life abounds in practices, institutions, and behaviors that would be quite inexplicable and idle ceremonies were it not for shared assumptions that, when made explicit and analyzed, are seen to be moral in nature. The fairly widely acknowledged notion of the "reasonable man," as well as the related notion of "consenting adults," implies a vast array of justifiable assumptions, among them the web of common moral principles. It is from this web that moral philosophies arise, and against which moral theories are in part tested.[7] The

---

7. By "in part" I mean that moral theories must, in the end, not conflict with our most fundamental and general pre-philosophical moral intuitions. There are, of course, other requirements of a moral theory, that it be internally consistent, broad in scope, applicable by the ordinary person, etc. This fact of human life may account for the phenomenon that nearly everyone takes his or her own moral opinion about something quite seriously, if not always reflectively. After all, in addition to the acquired cultural and social prejudices we are subject to, and which may vary from time to time and place to place, there is also a moral wellspring of principles, virtues, and values that can be traced to human nature itself, to the fact that we are rational beings, language bearers, and self-interested agents. Failure to understand the values implied by our nature, coupled with a failure to distinguish between behavior and meaning, leads often to cross-cultural moral assessments that are off the mark and compound conceptual confusion with normative error.

ethics of employment, beginning with the initial creation of the employment relationship, i.e., the agreed-to terms, is also grounded in the common moral web. And so we can apply not only common sense moral thinking to the area of employment, we can also apply the insights offered by fairly well developed moral theories.

EMPLOYMENT AND MORAL THEORIES

Now, how does all of this apply to the ethics employment at the level of abstraction, theoretically? Put generally, the terms of the employment agreement must be (i.e., are implicitly understood to be) offered by both sides in good faith, free of fraud, without threat of coercion, and open to acceptance, rejection, or possible revision or negotiation. These features are almost always taken for granted and become explicit only under special circumstances, or when, at some later date, conflict occurs and the original agreement is brought into question. The employment relationship is essentially a relationship of trade, with each side offering the other something of value in exchange, the most typical arrangement being some form of labor in exchange for a wage. The trade feature of the relationship means that employment is inherently tied to self-interest. That is, each side seeks to benefit from the trade, otherwise the proposed agreement would make no sense. Thus, the employment relationship has an inherently normative, indeed, moral feature, for it concerns human beings choosing so as to add value to their lives, recognizing that the other is doing likewise. For example, I choose to offer my labor in exchange for a certain wage, believing that I shall benefit therefrom, and offer what I believe the other will perceive as of benefit to him. And, just as I would see it as an injury or loss to myself were the other to misrepresent what he offered to me, so too must I recognize my misrepresenting what I offer as an injury to the other. My understandable resentment toward the other were he to misrepresent the offer and thus bring me loss or injury, means that I expected to not be so treated, and this expectation arises from the very nature of trade, that it generally serves to be mutually beneficial. But it could hardly have this feature if people were not generally forthright when trading.

This reciprocity feature implicit in the employment agreement is consistent with Kant's second formulation of the Categorical Imperative, commanding that one treat others as "ends in themselves," i.e., as like oneself in morally relevant ways. Genuine trade, trade befitting of human beings, Kant might say, is possible only among parties that acknowledge and respect one another's autonomy. Fraud, threat, distortion, coercion, and the like, corrupt and undermine the essentially moral basis of trade.

The self-interest feature of trade, of the employment relationship, makes the moral philosophy of Ethical Egoism relevant to employment ethics. Egoism, perhaps more appropriately, known as Moral Individualism, holds as its central principle that one ought to act so as to bring about one's own best (or enlightened or rational) self-interest.[8] Clearly, as one enters into an employment agreement, with so much typically at stake, it behooves each party to be thoughtful, prudent, and as knowledgeable of factors relevant to the context as possible, so as to maximize the securing of terms that are as beneficial to oneself as possible. From the employer's perspective, for instance, it would be prudent to consider an offer that would secure him the most return in productivity and profits with the lowest expenditure in labor costs. There may indeed be a "going wage" for the type of work offered, including typical benefits, to be adjusted by a variety of other factors, including particular working conditions, hours to be

8. The terms "best," "enlightened," and "rational" are to be understood in this essay as synonymous. The basic idea of Moral Individualism is that each individual human being flourishes or tends toward the realization of his/her potential as a human being just to the extent that he/she lives thoughtfully, intelligently, so as to live fully and happily. Moral Individualism sees the commonly recognized virtues of courage, honesty, generosity, prudence, patience, and such as not only definitive of human excellence, but also as essential elements of happiness, the good life.

worked, likelihood of continued employment, additional benefits, pay raises, etc., all open to bargaining.[9] The same considerations apply, mutatis mutandis, to any prospective employee. As in other aspects of life, there is no escaping the need for, and wisdom of, thoughtful consideration. Acting in one's own best interest means acting prudently and responsibly.

The "mutually beneficial" aspect of the employment relationship is consistent with the Utilitarian Principle, which praises actions in proportion to the happiness they produce. Employment brings about perceived and pursued benefits to both parties, not to mention in many cases to others, such as customers, and can thereby be seen as contributing to the "greater good." Granted, the principle of utility can be interpreted so as to obligate the party that has the greater advantage to give more than he may otherwise be willing to offer. However, such an interpretation, if employed on a widescale basis, would not only result in the overall decline of productivity, it would also undermine the free trade feature of the employment relationship, the feature that presupposes the moral autonomy of both parties. The terms of employment would no longer be determined by the rational and voluntary efforts of the parties; rather, an egalitarian calculus would prevail. Such is the case with the planned economies of socialist states, resulting in national bankruptcy as well as in the moral weakness of a citizenry that depends upon the state to make decisions that properly belong to the individual. On utilitarian grounds, then, the employment relationship as conceived in this essay is fully justified.

---

9. This assumes the moral context of a completely free exchange, without the interference of the state with its mandated regulations, minimum wage laws, overtime restrictions, etc. Clearly, the more state involvement here, the less freedom either prospective employer or employee has, and the less room there is for individual initiative, creativity, and responsibility for the terms of the relationship. Thus, the moral dimension of the employment relationship diminishes in direct proportion to state involvement.

The employment relationship is also a model of Social Contract Theory. According to this view, variously understood by thinkers such as Hobbes, Locke, and Rousseau, society comes into being by means of, and social, legal, and cultural rules are justified because of, the consent or agreement of the parties involved. Thus arises the idea of "consent of the governed," which, in terms of the employment relationship, means consent to the terms mutually agreed to. And, as in Social Contract Theory, the agreement defines the relationship, is binding, and is rationally grounded because the goal that motivates the autonomous agents to enter into the agreement is the expected benefit derived therefrom.

According to Theistic Ethics, as embodied in the Judeo-Christian-Moslem tradition, the employment relationship is as we have described. This is implicit in the Old Testament but made quite explicit in the New, where, in the Gospel according to Matthew, Jesus offers the parable of the vineyard owner in need of workers. The owner strikes a bargain with some men early in the day and makes the identical bargain several times later with other men, as the day progresses. At the end of the day, all of the workers discover that they have been paid the same sum, to which they had initially agreed, regardless of the hours worked. Those who worked the least were paid the same as those who labored for the entire day. Those hired earliest complained of unjust treatment, to which the vineyard owner replied, "Friend, I do thee no wrong; did'st not thou agree with me for a penny? . . . Is it not lawful for me to do what I will with mine own?" No doubt in contemporary American society the aggrieved workers would cry "exploitation" and take the owner to court. But, from a moral point of view, the complaint is groundless. No one entering into an agreement is entitled to more than the terms agreed to. No doubt Jesus had a loftier lesson in mind, but this story illustrates the main points stressed in this essay about the nature of the employment relationship. The story also underscores the practical wisdom of thinking for oneself in matters of employment. We can imagine the aggrieved workers making additional inquiries before entering into agreements thereafter, especially with the likes of the vineyard owner.

Given what was said earlier about the relationship between theory and practice, it should be no surprise that the principles of the major moral theories are fully consistent with common moral understanding and practice. The theories can illuminate us about the nature of employment, and can offer deeper and more sustained accounts of what ought to be done and why when various problems that arise in employment are complex or particularly significant. Consider, for a moment, the fact that there is widespread agreement, both at the commonsense level of morality, and theoretically, about the following: Given that the terms of the agreement that give birth to the employment relationship are voluntarily and mutually acceptable, and given that the agreement creates a reasonable expectation that each party will abide by the terms, it is prima facie wrong for either party to fail to meet the terms, and prima facie right that the terms be honored. This seems clear, obvious, and unobjectionable. In the end, it amounts to saying that one ought to keep one's word. Now, since there are terms to be kept on both sides, the ethics of employment necessarily require approaching employment questions and problems from two perspectives. Let's turn, then, to the question of how this moral base, supported as it is by moral theory, applies to some issues that arise in the area of employment.

There are some commonly held beliefs that employees are morally entitled to such things as a "fair" wage, job security, safe and healthful working conditions, as well as a variety of benefits, including sick leave, paid vacation, rest breaks, maternity leave with guaranteed re-employment, and so on. There are also beliefs concerning hiring and firing, such as nondiscrimination rights, equal pay for equal work, advance notice before termination, severance pay, and so on. These topics merit discussion.

HIRING AND FIRING

The employment relationship begins when a bargain is struck, when the terms of employment are agreed to. The question arises, "Are there moral constraints within which an employer must operate when it comes to hiring and to letting an employee go?" In other words, may an employer hire and fire "at will"? This question usually means, "May an employer hire whomever he wishes for whatever reasons and fire an employee whenever he wishes and for whatever reasons, without violating morality?" If so, then an employer may discriminate on the basis of race, gender, sexual preference, and so on, and may fire an employee to make room for, say, a relative, or in favor of someone whose looks the employer prefers. From the perspective of all the major moral theories, the answer to this question is "No," but with qualification.

Just as an employer clearly has a right not to hire anyone at all, not to offer work in the first place, she also has a right to hire whomever she wishes and for whatever reasons. However, the conceptual preconditions that the employment agreement be free of coercion, hoax, or fraud, morally preclude an employer from advertising a job opportunity publicly, knowing that some otherwise qualified applicants will not be seriously considered because they do not meet the employer's personal, extra-qualifications preference(s).

For example, should an employer advertise a job opening for, say, sales clerk at his store, knowing that he will not hire from a minority group, then he ought morally to make this clear.[10] Otherwise, quali-

---

10. It would, of course, be illegal today to do this. The point here is that, from a strictly moral point of view, an employer's job offer is an extension of his right to property. And, just as he may or may not sell that property to whomever he wishes, because, for example, he does not want a particular person or kind of person to have that property, so too may he refuse to hire whomever he wishes, provided that the preconditions of no fraud, coercion, or deceit are met, as discussed in this chapter.

fied minorities, having reasonable expectation of being seriously considered upon application, would be victims of deliberate deceit. The advertised opportunity would, to that extent, be fraudulent. Unless otherwise advertised, all candidates with the job-related qualifications ought to be seriously considered. Of course, in actual life, many employers consider, to varying degrees of seriousness, all manner of personal characteristics that may not be strictly job related, such as age, race, sex, physical appearance, and so on. No doubt, as well, many employers sometimes hire in favor of their preferences, and can do so with impunity, not to mention the absurdity of expecting an employer to advertise all of the non-job-relevant preferences an employer might have with respect to an employee. So, this requirement that the agreement be nonfraudulent seems to be a moot point. But consider that the question here is what an employer ought to do, not what in fact some may do or have done.

Many, perhaps most, people believe that an employer seeking to hire ought to be guided only by the job description and the extent to which applicants meet the qualifications. Thus, the "most qualified" applicant ought to be hired. After all, this is what one would want for oneself, should one be a candidate. Anything less seems to be making significant decisions on irrelevant grounds. But is this necessarily so? From the employer's point of view, the job requirements per se may not be all that matters. Certainly she is looking for someone who can do the job, but she may also desire an employee that has a pleasant personality, or a quiet demeanor, or one that does not smell of tobacco or perfume. The employer may be considering the social aspects of the work environment and the effect that a prospective employee, however otherwise qualified, may have on co-workers, or on the employer herself, not to mention on customers or clients, vendors, and others who might interact with the employee as a representative of the employer's business.

For obvious reasons, employers are as a rule guided primarily by the need to fill an opening with the most qualified applicant, and, as a rule the specified job requirements include relevant experience, skills, knowledge, training, and education. But, depending on the position to be filled, certain qualifications may outweigh others, and rarely are applicants identical in all relevant respects. Furthermore, it may well be that the "most qualified" applicant lacks a sense of humor, has an annoying mannerism, or an otherwise distracting or unpleasant characteristic. Depending on the context, this may be a minor or a serious consideration. The employer is likely in the best position to determine this. Thus, the employer must have latitude and discretion, though he may be guided by the job requirements. Were the employer morally bound to hire the "most qualified" no matter what, this would, on at least some occasions, result in the employer hiring someone he judged to be a less promising prospect for his business than a "less qualified" candidate. However, this would contradict the very purpose of hiring someone to begin with, namely, to find someone whom the employer deemed most suitable for the job. On analysis, it is not so evident what the boundaries are of a relevant qualification, much less that an employer ought to hire solely on this basis.

The conclusions reached thus far are supported by appeal to the nature of the employment relationship, and reinforced when considered from the perspective of the applicant. By nature, both employer and employee expect to gain from the employment, else agreement to terms would be irrational. Suppose that the employer is offering what would otherwise be attractive job-related terms, such as an attractive wage, benefits, hours, etc., the counterpart to job qualifications. In other words, the employer, by her offer of terms, has met the job-related qualifications. Is the applicant morally bound to accept the terms? Suppose, further, that, despite the terms, the applicant finds certain features of the prospective employment personally distasteful or otherwise not meeting his personal preferences, such as the employer is very ugly, has noticeable body odor, is a bit loud and brusque, or some such qualities, or the place of employment is unattractive, other employees are seemingly unfriendly, traffic to work would be burdensome, parking a challenge, or many other possible unwelcome factors. Under some such description, suppose that an applicant declined a job offer in favor of another job with less pay, fewer benefits, etc., that is, a job with less qualifications because it met his personal non-job-related preferences. Clearly, this is well within the person's rights. It would be absurd to hold that the applicant must accept a job simply because the terms offered met his expectations, met his "qualifications." By parity of reasoning it follows that an employer is not morally bound to hire the "most qualified" applicant.

When it comes to terminating an employee and ending the employment relationship, the employer has much less latitude than with hiring. This is because the employee, though having no right to the job as an applicant (the employer could have decided, without moral blame, not to hire any of the applicants after all), does have a right, based on reasonable expectation established by the employment agreement, to remain employed so long as she meets her end of the agreement and so long as the business continues to require her services. The employer may not, morally, fire at will. However, should it eventuate that the services of the employee are no longer required, the employer is not morally bound to continue the relationship, else he would become slave to his own employee! He is, though, morally bound to serve advance notice as early as is possible and prudent. This obligation is reciprocal: the same applies to an employee about to quit her job. It is prima facie wrong for either employer or employee to terminate the employment relationship without reasonable advance notice, since the welfare of the other to whom one is bound by moral agreement, is at stake. Such eventualities (among others) can be anticipated and ought, if feasible, to be addressed by the terms of the original agreement. Prudent forethought can prevent much avoidable grief.

FAIR WAGE AND BENEFITS

From the perspective of the employee, the amount of pay or wage in return for his/her labor or services is likely the most important feature of the employment agreement. The principal reason for seeking employment is, after all, to earn money, which is the principal means of acquiring much, if not most, of what one needs and values for survival and quality living. It is commonly believed that every person is entitled to a fair wage. The idea here is that persons have a right to a decent life, to at least the minimum that is required for survival, and then some, should resources be available. What counts as just with respect to the distribution of resources is explored in the area of philosophy called Distributive or Economic Justice. It has been argued that an economically just society is one where each citizen receives an equal share of the society's resources, or one where each citizen is guaranteed at least the basic necessities, or one where each receives a share proportionate to his productive input, as determined by market demand.[11] Depending upon one's view, an economically just society will be somewhere on a continuum of socioeconomic models from laissez faire, to varying degrees of welfare statism, to communism. Now, regardless of the merits of the various positions taken on the questions of Distributive Justice, an issue that certainly exceeds the scope of our present inquiry, it is safe to say that the more one's model of Distributive Justice includes a guarantee of wages and benefits, prior to the employment agreement, the less there will be of the moral feature of employment. That is, the more that what would have counted as the terms to be negotiated are presupposed, perhaps even coded into law and backed by threat of

---

11. For a brief overview of three positions on this question, including a defense of the social-welfare state, see Trudy Govier, "The Right to Eat and the Duty to Work," *Philosophy of the Social Sciences*, vol. 5 (1975). For a brief defense of the free market view on this question, see Irving Kristol's *Two Cheers for Capitalism* (New York: Basic Books, 1978).

force, the less room there will be for careful and deliberate choice by either party.[12]

How is a fair wage to be determined? Indeed, how is a minimum wage determined? In the simplest sense of the term "minimum," such a wage would be the lowest that a prospective employee would be willing to accept, and this would vary from person to person. If Jones is willing to work for a lower wage than is Smith, an employer could hardly be called unfair, or unjust, in hiring Jones, anymore than Jones could be accused of unjustly depriving Smith of the job by accepting a lower wage.

Further, the idea of a fair wage, understood as anything other than the wage freely agreed to, is a conceptual error. The wage that an employee is willing to work for depends upon a host of other factors that the employee (ought to and usually) has taken into account: in contrast with available employment options, the hours to be worked, the prospects of long-term employment, the prospects for advancement, pay raises, fringe-benefits such as a retirement plan, health plan, vacation, sick days, distance from home to work, conditions at the workplace, including safety features, conveniences, possible social relationship, and other factors will determine a fair wage—that is, the wage that a person will be willing to accept. Thus, $10 per hour, everything considered, may be acceptable to one person, a boon to another, and woefully inadequate for yet a third. No one can determine in advance, prior to offers being tendered, what a fair wage will be for any job. We can, of course, answer the empirical question of what the going rate is for many jobs, but that fact tells us only

---

12. Rather strong support of the view that increasing state involvement undermines the volitional, and thus, moral feature of employment, comes from France, where recently, companies that violated the zero-tolerance, no-overtime-work law faced fines sufficient to disincline employers and employees from agreeing to mutually beneficial overtime arrangements. As a result of the inhibition created by threat of fines, some companies in France are finding it hard to compete with companies from other countries that have no overtime restrictions.

what people are typically, or on average, being paid for that kind of work. Such facts have little, if any, moral implications.

In terms of the basic features of employment described above, a just or fair wage would be one that each side agrees to, so long as there is no misrepresentation, fraud, or coercion, just as a fair or just price for some property one wishes to sell is the price that seller and buyer agree to. This does not mean that each side will be equally benefited by the exchange, but a resulting inequality does not mean that either party had acted unjustly. One might have acted prematurely, without sufficient forethought, or acted impulsively, or ignorantly, or perhaps unknowable factors were at work to account for the inequality. Regardless, so long as the terms agreed to come by way of bargaining in good faith, one cannot say that the wage is unjust. Now, it may be indecently low, meaning that the employer may be quite able to offer more without sacrifice to herself, but instead refuses to pay any more than a desperate prospective employee is willing to accept. Some may call such a situation coercive. After all, the worker has no power, no alternatives, is at the mercy of the employer, and the subsequent working conditions may likely amount to exploitation. Such circumstances fuel talk of workers' rights, the idea that, given the typically disadvantageous position of the employee relative to the employer, the worker is morally entitled to certain special consideration, including such benefits as health and safety provisions. In other words, were the worker to actually be on equal bargaining terms, these benefits would be among those that he/she would bargain for. On this reasoning, it is only the difference in power, favoring the employer, that accounts for the lack of benefits that the employee would otherwise enjoy.[13]

This view certainly has merit and, given the exigencies of supply and demand, many workers, particularly the relatively unskilled, have little to offer as bargaining chips. They are, so to speak, at the mercy

13. For a defense of workers' rights, see P. H. Werhane, *Persons, Rights, and Corporations* (Englewood Cliffs, N.J.: Prentice Hall, 1985).

of employers. No wonder that the acquiring of education and of marketable skills is so much a part of common wisdom. The very concept of a "marketable" skill suggests that those workers whose skills are in demand are more likely to secure desired benefits than those without such skills. This appears to be an inherent feature of free markets and of human life, not of the employment relationship as such, and only an external force such as government mandates could make it otherwise. Thus, the appeal to a special set of workers' rights based on the power differential between employer and employee has the following oddity: The "rights" exist just to the extent that the power differential exists and in direct proportion to the difference in power. In other words, the rights would be going in and out of existence and would fluctuate in force with shifts in the market. It should also be pointed out that the converse of the power differential is also possible: An employer unable to offer sufficiently attractive terms may have to settle for a less skilled, experienced, or desirable applicant.

Furthermore, even in those circumstances where the employee is at the mercy of the employer, it is an error to call the terms or the conditions unjust, however deplorable the conditions. The employer who is capable of offering more but refuses to is acting within his rights, and within the boundaries of moral obligation. He owes the employee(s) only what was agreed to; he is not (we assume) responsible for the employee's desperate circumstances, and he is no more obligated to pay beyond what is agreed to than he is obligated to offer a job in the first place. If an employer were morally bound to offer a particular wage, then, at least to that extent—which would be considerable—the fundamental nature of the employment relationship as described earlier would be so altered that we could not call it an agreement at all. In short, the free exchange feature of the employment relationship would be lost, just as if, in the market, one were prohibited from deciding for oneself the value or worth of a product or service, and from bargaining over the price. One casualty of this would be the elimination of each party's acting prudently, intelligently, and thoughtfully, about a matter of significance to his life. The view that there could be a morally obligatory wage or other employment benefit would, ironically, rob the employment relationship of the very feature that makes it a moral matter in the first place!

Many people believe that there is a minimal standard of living tolerable in a society with sufficient resources, and that, at very least, employers ought to offer a wage no less than would provide the worker with such a living. On this view, a fair or decent wage is presumably determined by the cost of living within a community or a society. Something along these lines is the rationale for our national minimum wage law. But the guarantee of such a wage prior to an employment agreement is not consistent with the nature of employment in its basic moral sense. Such a guarantee would be a politically mandated, coercive action, requiring state involvement. Our concern here is with the moral dimension of employment, which presupposes that the terms are a matter ultimately to be decided between the prospective employer and employee.

Everything said above with respect to wages applies as well to benefits. In years past, anything in addition to the wage, such as overtime pay, vacation pay, insurance, and the like, was referred to as a "fringe" benefit, underscoring the primacy of the wage as of value to the employee. Given the growth of wealth in recent decades, the influence of labor unions, and the expansion of public employment, which includes extra-wage benefits as part of a total employment package, it is now commonly expected that at least some benefits in addition to the wage will be offered by employers. This, of course, makes the idea of a "fair" wage even less definitive. Clearly, the more that an employer is willing to offer in the form of a wage, the less she will be willing and able to offer in the form of benefits, and vice-versa, since benefits, like wages, are a cost of labor to be assumed by the employer. There can be no ideal or objectively determined balance of wage and benefits apart from a context that includes particular persons, places, and circumstances, all of which are bound to vary.

Now, to say that there is no morally well-grounded claim to workers' rights, and that an employer does not have a moral obligation to provide anything more than the market will bear, does not mean that employees are never exploited, or that such employers are free of moral blame. Morality includes much more than rights, duties, and obligations. In particular, morality consists, perhaps essentially, in the expression of virtues and avoidance of vices. Among the virtues are charity, compassion, and kindness to others. These human excellences are not duties such as others can be said to have a right to them from others, but they are constitutive of human character and expressive of human goodness. Thus, failure to be virtuous when called upon is cause not for punishment or redress, but for moral censure. Failure to act virtuously does not so much bring upon one judgment of guilt as it does judgment of shame.

Now, the idea of workers' rights is likely motivated by genuine sympathy for the plight of others, and the tendency to respond in the language of rights is understandable but misplaced. There is indeed cause for moral outrage at exploitation, whether in employment or elsewhere, but the moral failure is the lack of charity, compassion, kindness, human decency. The language of rights and duties has the practical advantage of offering justification for legal protection, backed by threat of force in the form of punishment such as fines or incarceration. By comparison, moral censure typically fails as a catalyst for change, ironically, all the more so as morality collapses into law and the difference becomes obscured. Such has been the direction of our culture, of most social democracies: the more that morality is legislated, the less genuine morality will there be.

JOB SECURITY

Without doubt one of the most disruptive and personally threatening events for most people would be to lose a job. A recurring complaint aimed at "corporate America" is that it treats employees as expendable, and that the disruptions caused by downsizing, plant closing, relocation, and mass layoffs in the name of "the bottom line," are an undue hardship on ordinary workers. A theme of the recently emerging "communitarian" view is that companies have an obligation to the communities in which they do business, including an obligation not to relocate or to practice large-scale layoffs. Workers have a "right" to job security, it is often argued. Setting aside the more general question of the obligations, if any, that a company has to the community in which it operates, we can address the narrower question, "Does an employer have an obligation to see to the continued employment of her employee(s)?" Does an employee have a right to job security?

Clearly, a worker has a reasonable expectation of continued employment so long as she meets the terms of the employment agreement, and in this sense she does have job security. This seems to be implicit in the original agreement. Thus, if the employee is meeting her end of the terms, it would be wrong for an employer to dismiss her without just cause. As part of common understanding until quite recently, a person was thought to be secure in her job to the extent that she was a productive worker, loyal to the company, honest, and otherwise an asset to the business. Secure, that is, so long as the employer can afford to honor the terms of the employment agreement. A job is only as secure as the business is thriving. Lately, the idea has been gaining currency that workers have a right to be secure in their jobs, to be free of the worry of losing their jobs to the whim of the employer or to downturns in the economy. As noted earlier, an employer may not morally dismiss an employee without just cause, but the guarantee of security, independent of factors such as the health of the business, would essentially turn the employer into an indentured servant, thus undermining the voluntary feature necessary to the employment relationship. To say that the employer must continue employing a worker "no matter what," is logically equivalent to saying that the employee must continue working for the employer "no matter what," which of course is absurd. Should the employee get a better job offer elsewhere, or learn that relocating would likely improve her career prospects, no one would seriously argue that it would be immoral of him to terminate her employment.

An employer can hardly be morally expected to provide an employee continued employment for a position that is no longer serving the needs of the employer. In this sense, a job is only as secure as there is a market demand for it—just as a business is secure only to the extent that there is a market demand for its products or services. Without customers who are willing to pay for the product or services, there would be no need for workers. To the extent that one person's job is guaranteed secure through, say, protective legislation, someone else's job, or freedom, will be curtailed.

HEALTH AND SAFETY

Matters of health and safety in the workplace ought to be major considerations to both employees and employers. Some might argue that an employer has a moral obligation to see to the health and safety of her employees. Since the employee is under the direction and supervision of the employer, is working on the premises of the owner, usually using the tools and equipment of the owner, it is up to the employer to see to it that the working conditions, including the equipment, are safe. Additionally, the employer is generally more knowledgeable about such matters relevant to her industry and is therefore in a better position to anticipate dangers than are employees. There is, after all, a prima facie duty to avoid harm to others, and health and safety protection are clearly preventive measures.

According to this view, the employer is morally obligated to provide a safe and healthful working environment.

On the other hand, appealing to the nature of the employment relationship, it can be argued that the employer has no obligation apart from the terms to which he has agreed. If anyone should attend to matters of health and safety, it is the employee herself, since it is her own welfare and interests that are at stake. It would be imprudent of an employee to assume that the employer will see to these matters. The view that it is the employer's duty, not the employee's, misplaces the burden, discourages caution, and thus puts the employee at even greater risk than otherwise. As for the prima facie duty to avoid injury, this is a negative, not a positive, duty. It admonishes one from acting in ways that, if avoidable, bring harm or injury to innocent others, unless a more morally compelling duty cannot be met without such injury. In other words, this duty does not require that the employer provide anything special by way of health and safety protection.

All this said, there is nonetheless very good reason for the employer to see to health and safety in the workplace. It is in the employer's best interest to provide a working environment free of undue risk of injury or illness, since productivity is directly and negatively affected by injury and illness. Just as it makes good sense for a prospective employee to assess the safety conditions of the workplace as part of his consideration of the merits of the job, so too does it make sense for the employer to attend to risk of injury and threat to health in the workplace of his business.

But health, safety, and risk are relative and must be understood contextually. Different industries pose different dangers, and to varying degrees. Even with elaborate precautions, some jobs are inherently more dangerous than others. Over time, various industries have gathered data, assessed risks, and provided "industry standards" to inform and guide the decisions and behaviors of those within the industry. Understandably, these standards must themselves be adjusted to relevant differences in location, as well as to changes in and accessibility to relevant technology, new discoveries, and economic conditions. Generally speaking, lowering the risk of injury or disease is technology dependent, and on a continuum from somewhat effective to "state of the art." Additionally, the more effective the protection, usually the greater the cost. It is also a fact of life that some people are willing to run greater risks than others, and to assess risks differently.

In other words, though both employee and employer have a vested interest in the safety of the working environment, the degree of interest, as well as the degree of risk that anyone is willing to take or expect others to take, cannot be quantified or predicted. Thus, even with industry standards, individual preference, assessment, and judgment are called for. One prospective employee may be willing to run a greater risk for the same pay than another, or to perceive the risk differently. One employer may assess the productivity implications of certain preventive measures as more promising than another, and so on.

What all of this means is that, though neither employer nor employee have rights against or duties toward one another over and above the employment agreement, they can and ought to include health and safety considerations among the specific terms of the employment contract, if there is special reason to do so. It should be noted here that there are certain widely expected, because common, standards of health and safety for workers in various industries, and for the most part these are already generally provided by employers, such as adequate heating, lighting, and ventilation. Over time, given technological advances, greater knowledge, and reduced costs resulting from economies of scale in response to increased demand, what at one time may have been prohibitive (and thus rare) health and safety protection, may become reasonable and customary. What passes for safe today, or in this or that industry, may, from some future vantage point, be seen as deplorable or reckless by comparison. In any event, the employer has an obligation to provide working conditions that meet common expectations, or to inform prospective employees if they do not. But, since continued advances and new knowledge seem ever unfolding, there may always be thresholds, gray areas, about which thoughtful people may disagree, as to what is reasonable or customary.

ORGANIZED LABOR

Given the generally social tendency of human beings, especially the tendency of people with like circumstances to associate with one another, it is hardly a surprise that workers would find it in their interests to associate as workers. Such associations can take various forms, from loosely structured, informal socials, to clubs, to unions with dues, elected representatives, and bargaining power. There is strength in numbers, in solidarity, in sharing resources, ideas, and problems, and doing so in an organized way is inherently more productive, efficient, and effective, than to do so haphazardly. So, some degree of labor organizing would seem inevitable, especially as the number of employees in a business increases. It is not the case that employee organizations are inherently adversarial with respect to management. Indeed, both employer and employee can benefit from organized labor since the organization can serve as a resource of information, and as a vehicle of communication between employer and employees, which can enhance relationships between labor and management.

The employment relationship typically continues over an extended period of time, during which many factors affecting employment are likely to change, and to raise employee concerns. Through an employee organization, workers can more effectively voice employment concerns and increase their influence on management decisions. All of this can be accomplished without adversity and to the mutual benefit of employer and employee. Under conditions of good faith communication, where all parties are willing to listen and are resolved to work together toward mutually agreeable solutions, it is likely that participants will consider matters from other points of view, thus reducing the chance of misunderstanding, resentment, and entrenchment, which result in warring camps.

Admittedly, this view of the employment relationship runs counter to the widely held attitude that workers must unite "against" their employers, lest they be exploited in the employer's greedy pursuit of profits. Historical appeals to the working conditions of the early industrial period support this perception, as do appeals to the advances made by labor subsequent to forceful strategies by labor unions in the first half of the twentieth century. But, even granting this interpretation of labor history, the apparent premise underlying the common attitude is that the employment relationship is inherently adversarial. This premise does not hold up under analysis.

However compelling its historical origins, the adversarial view too rigidly identifies people with their roles and tends to stereotype these as well. It treats accidental features of employer and employee as though they were essential features of the employment relationship. This error creates the very division that the adversarial view holds to be inherent in the employment relationship. In other words, the common attitude begs the question.

We saw earlier that the employment relationship is essentially a matter of morality, which requires that we treat people as persons who are rational and able to make choices for themselves. There is nothing inherent in one's social or economic class, or in one's employment circumstances, that precludes one from treating others morally. It is simply social or economic prejudice to assume, as does the adversarial view, that employers are inherently evil, i.e., unwilling to treat employees with moral respect. Immorality is a feature of individual human beings, not of a social class. Without doubt, some employers are stingy, disrespectful, exploitative, and uncaring. But not all. Those who are, have come by it on their own, not because they are employers. Likely the same persons, as employees, would continue to be stingy, disrespectful, exploitative, and uncaring, as no doubt many employees are. Human faults and frailties find a home in every social and economic class.

In a number of industries, such as mining, steel, auto, and trucking, unions have become the predominant mode of organization for workers in various parts of the country. The exact nature of a union is not easy to define and distinguish from other forms of labor organization, but generally a union appears to be a relatively highly organized association of workers, complete with dues for membership, a hierarchically structured administration with elected positions, and agents who represent the membership in bargaining for wages and benefits. The larger and more powerful a union, the greater is employee leverage in bargaining for desired wages and benefits, mainly because the threat of work stoppage, or strike, poses considerable disruption of commerce within the industry or business.

Many people believe that, short of government mandates, unions are the best assurance that workers will be treated fairly.[14] It is also widely believed that unions are a major cause of the improvement of working conditions, wages, and benefits, though there is dispute about the overall desirability of the bargaining power of unions.

For example, it has been argued that unions ultimately work against the consumer because the additional cost of labor secured by union bargaining results in higher prices of goods and services to consumers.[15] What this means is that the gains to union employees

14. Today labor organizations are highly regulated and protected by a considerable body of legislation. For a discussion of the history of unionized labor and regulations, see T. R. Machan, "Some Philosophical Aspects of National Labor Policy," *Harvard Journal of Law and Public Policy* 4 (1981): 67–160.

15. For an elaboration of this point, see J. T. Bennet, "Does a Higher Wage Really Mean You Are Better Off?" (Springfield, Va.: National Institute for Labor Relations Research, 1985).

may come at the expense of other workers.[16] Much the same could be said about strikes, which effectively curtail or altogether stop production.

A strike suspends the employment relationship, with the end of compelling the employer, by virtue of economic pressure, to agree to certain terms. On its face this seems inconsistent with the original description of the employment agreement, which requires that there be no coercion. However, this requirement applies to the origination of the agreement.

Once an employment relationship exists, a union is in place, and bargaining reaches an impasse, a strike is the temporary termination of the relationship, not a violation of the terms, unless the terms of the original agreement included a no-strike provision. Apart from this, there is nothing in principle wrong with employees refusing to work, and circumstances are conceivable where this would be the most effective and reasonable strategy for workers. Such a strategy amounts to the workers quitting, terminating the employment relationship. But, under these circumstances the employer is hardly morally bound to rehire the employees. Unless the employer has breached the terms originally agreed to, or has otherwise acted fraudulently or coercively, a work stoppage is equivalent to quitting one's job. An employer's obligations to an employee end with the termination of the employment relationship.

Everything said thus far is within the context of morality. There exist a host of laws and regulations relevant to employment, unions, and the legal rights of workers that may or may not be consistent with the moral view sketched in this essay. A considerable body of literature exists that explores the relationship between employment laws and morality, as well as the social, political, and economic

16. See William Hutt, *The Strike Threat System: The Economic Consequences of Collective Bargaining* (Indianapolis, Ind.: Liberty Press, 1975).

implications of protective legislation. A final word: Since the employment relationship is essentially moral in nature, employment legislation that diminishes the freedom and responsibility of individuals to make decisions regarding their own welfare is morally questionable.

CHAPTER TWO

Toward a Personalist Workplace Ethic

Gregory M. A. Gronbacher
Rev. Robert A. Sirico

THIS CHAPTER ATTEMPTS to derive a coherent ethic of work from two main intellectual sources—Christian social teaching and free-market economic theory. Such an ethic would not only be logical but also relevant to today's issues and dilemmas. With this as the goal, this chapter sets out to explain these sources and demonstrate how their meeting points in human action, liberty, and dignity serve as the foundation for a meaningful philosophy of work. In particular, this paper will rely on Christian social teaching in its expression in Catholic social doctrine found in the papal encyclicals and the personalist philosophical and theological tradition generated by such thinkers as Emmanuel Mounier, Emil Brunner, and Karol Wojtyla (Pope John Paul II). The conjoining of personalism, Christian social teaching, and free-market economies is treated as controversial by some, particularly those scholastics within the theological community. This chapter will demonstrate that these intellectual traditions compliment, rather than contradict, each other, and that Catholic social teaching and personalism can provide a moral and anthropological basis for better understanding the truth of a market economy.

THE NATURE OF HUMAN WORK

How one defines work, obviously, will determine how one understands work. In an effort to define work, several distinctions prove useful. The first is the distinction between human action in general and work. By human action in general we refer to all human activity, voluntary and involuntary—everything from blinking to choosing a career. Action in this sense is the broadest category of the dynamism of human life. This broad category of general human action, therefore, contains within it other necessary distinctions. These subsequent distinctions include voluntary and involuntary actions of the person. Work is, therefore, a subspecies of voluntary human actions.

Work is any intentional human action, the performance of which requires cost to self and is aimed at a productive end. Work is therefore delineated from leisure activities that are also voluntary and purposeful, yet engaged in for reasons that are not necessarily strictly limited to production—such as enjoyment, relaxation, and even creative efforts not undertaken for material profit or the satisfaction of human need. Even these distinctions, admittedly, cannot explain all human behavior. Some behavior blurs such distinctions to the degree they are no longer useful. One need only think about the artist who makes a living from creative leisure to see this point.

In addition to philosophy, theology has much to say about the nature of human work. Work appears in the first few lines of the Jewish and Christian sacred texts. In the book of Genesis we open to the story of the world's creation by God. God's generative and fertile love produces the whole of creation from nothing.[1] Creation, therefore, can be understood as an ongoing work of love from the Creator. Again, admittedly, discussing the creation as work has its limitations. God expected no profit from his creation. God created

---

1. This concept is referred to as *creatio ex nihilo,* or creation from nothing, implying that before God acted to make the cosmos, nothing existed except God.

without cost to self. Strictly speaking, then, God's initial act of creation of the universe is one of those actions that transcends strict distinctions, yet at the same time merits being considered as a form of work.

Yet, even though we may not strictly speak of God's creation as work in the limited sense in which we wish to employ the term, we can gain several meaningful insights from this account of the origins of mankind. We see in the creation stories of Genesis that men and women are created in God's own image and likeness. The phrase "in his image and likeness" is usually taken to mean that men and women share certain traits or faculties in common with God, yet we share these traits only analogously. Foundational to these shared characteristics is the notion that we are created as persons and therefore share in the personal nature of God. By "person" we refer to a subjective, relational, conscious, choosing, and affective being whose capacities include rationality, aesthetic appreciation, love, and even self-reflection.

Our creation as persons also implies that we share in one of the most evident aspects of God's own nature—creativity. We are co-creators with God. There is an impulse latent in all living beings that orients them toward the assimilation of matter that preserves, renews, and strengthens their vital energy. Indeed, one of the more fundamental aspects of human existence is our ability to adapt for survival. In order to survive, human beings must engage in the activities of production and consumption.

The Creator has given ample provision for human need in nature, but we must interact with our environment to utilize these resources. This process of utilization begins with basic elements of life-sustaining activity: appropriation of food and then, at a later stage, tool-making for increased efficiency in harvesting and the construction of shelter. This process continues to build upon itself, resulting in the development of new and more effective means for increasing the utilization of scarce resources.

God, therefore, creates the world from nothing, creates man in his own image, gives the world to man and his care, and requires as a part of this stewardship that man realize the *imago dei* through exercising his creativity in work. Resounding throughout this Genesis account is the voice of God proclaiming all this as good. Work, therefore, appears to be part of the original plan of God for mankind.

This view of the created order, specifically the goodness of the material world, has not been accepted without controversy, even within the Christian tradition. Early in the history of Christianity a movement developed that regarded the material world as fundamentally evil, viciously created by a demi-god. This movement came to be known as Gnosticism. The Gnostic impulse has surfaced and resurfaced under many guises throughout Christian history.

Orthodox Christian teaching has always rejected Gnosticism because it denies God's Incarnation in Christ. The Incarnation, accordingly, represents the manifestation of God's presence in history, in the person of Jesus Christ. Christian doctrine holds that it is through the Incarnation that God has reconciled the world (cosmos) to Himself (Col. 1:15–23; John 1:1–14; 2 Cor. 5:16–19). The implications of this throughout history have produced mixed reactions among Christians. In the second century the Docetists believed that Jesus was divine but refused to believe that he was fully human. In the fourth century, for example, the Arians believed that Jesus was the highest created being but refused to grant him equality with the Father.

In the face of these distinct views, the universal Christian Church agreed at the Council of Nicea (A.D. 325) that Jesus Christ was both God *and* man. If Jesus is true God and true man, then authentic anthropology is Christology. In the words of the Second Vatican Council and John Paul II, it is "Christ the Redeemer" who "fully reveals man to himself."[2]

2. Cf. Second Vatican Ecumenical Council, Pastoral Constitution on the

The root conflict over the morality of the free market and entrepreneurial vocation derives from denigration of the Incarnation and
skepticism over the goodness of the material order. This misgiving
stems from a Gnostic-inspired view that sees the material world as
evil and opposed to spiritual development. Work, according to such
a worldview, can only be seen as inherently flawed and a cause of
suffering.

Pope John Paul II, building on insights from traditional Christian-
tiy, provides us with an excellent alternative view of work. He reads
Genesis and states:

> Man has to subdue the earth and dominate it, because as the "image
> of God" he is a person, that is to say, a subjective being capable of
> acting in a planned and rational way, capable of deciding about him-
> self, and with a tendency to self-realization. *As a person, man is there-
> fore the subject of work.*[3]

Human action is the primary epistemological key to understanding
the person and, therewith, the human condition. Active persons
create new means of satisfying their needs. But what does it mean
to "create" or to be "creative"? "To create" means to make something
of value that did not previously exist. This ability is a capacity reserved
only for persons. Indeed, while some animals make things (beavers
make dams, for example), they follow instinct and not rational deliberation, which is foundational to human creativity. To create, in other
words, means that we must choose to be creative. While human
persons do not exhibit the same kind of creativity as God (the ability
to create something from nothing), nonetheless, because of their

---

Church in the Modern World *Gaudium et Spes*, 22, AAS 58 (1966): 1042–43. John
Paul II, Encyclical Letter *Redemptor Hominis* (March 4, 1979), nos. 8.1–8.2.

    3. John Paul II, Encyclical Letter *Laborem Exercens* (September 14, 1981), no.
6.2.

likeness to the Creator (*imago Dei*), they are capable of exercising creative powers.

When we think of human creativity, however, we often think only of people who work in the realm of ideas. Or, we think of those who work in the fine arts such as a sculptor or a musician. Creativity is a central aspect of human existence because it is an integral component of human action. Everyday experience shows that people create things in order to fulfill their needs. Therefore, in a broad sense, work is creative and evidences man's creativity.

In the process of fulfilling our needs, we search for ways—often new ways—of satisfying our needs. People must be creative because every need is unique. They cannot simply mimic the actions of others. The same needs, in addition, arise in diverse situations and circumstances and thus require different responses. Creativity grows through responding to human need.

To create something requires interacting with the external world—it requires action.[4] Hence, creativity cannot be separated from creative action, which is its expression. Attaining sufficient knowledge and ability to satisfy basic needs is only possible by first imagining how the need can be met, second by choosing to meet that need, and third by having the freedom to act upon that choice. Since human action utilizes these three elements, all human action is creative, at least to the extent that it is truly aimed at meeting needs.[5]

Far from being only a small segment of people's lives, then, creativity is the central expression of human personhood. Any economic, social, or political system that does not afford persons the freedom

---

4. It is often said, of course, that people *create* something merely when they imagine it, even when that imagination has no effect on the world around them (as, for example, when an artist imagines a piece of sculpture). Yet such an imagining is more appropriately an act than an action, because it has no direct effect on the world. Creation, then, is not the same as the imaginative act that precedes action. Put simply, creativity may require but is not encompassed by a *vivid imagination*.

5. Action that creates or aims to create need is motivated by disvalue. That kind of action is rightly considered to be destructive rather than creative.

to express their creativity in action diminishes their personhood. The ability to develop our subjectivity through work means that work can be part of the genuine development of the human person. Entrepreneurship, in addition, is a calling that mirrors the work of God by sharing in His ongoing creative efforts. An entrepreneur is a kind of *impresario*, one who organizes numerous factors and points them toward production. This creative aspect of the entrepreneur is akin to God's creative activity seen in Genesis. The entrepreneur participates in the call to productivity that is universal to the human race.

The Christian life, as we have already mentioned, necessarily encompasses the material order—including the world of business and finance—by virtue of the creation and Incarnation. The vocation of the entrepreneur to help build the kingdom of God through producing goods that increase societal well-being is an honorable calling.

Work expresses who we are, what we are, and what we believe. Just as the created order, God's work, expresses His character (Ps. 19:1–6), so our work makes visible our invisible spiritual nature. It shows our character, just as certainly as good works make known the presence of faith in the heart of one who professes it (James 2:18). In work, we reflect the image of our Maker (Gen. 1:26), for He too works (Gen. 2:2; John 5:17), and at the moment of our creation He commanded us to work.[6]

We are created in the image and likeness of God, and that means we are called to participate productively in the created order. This creativity is fundamental to all vocations, as is work.

Through work man must earn his daily bread and contribute to the continual advance of science and technology and, above all, to elevating unceasingly the cultural and moral level of the society within which he lives in community with those who belong to the same

6. Beisner, *Prosperity and Poverty*, 29.

family. And work means any activity of man, whether manual or intellectual, whatever its nature or circumstances.[7]

Creative participation implies a right to work. The right to work, however, is not necessarily the right to a particular job or form of employment. The right to work, rather, is understood broadly in that all persons have the right to productive activity undertaken for the benefit of providing for their needs and the needs of their family. This work may be in the employment of another, on a farm, in a factory, or in some other manner that is incorporated into the larger productive process of society.

In order to carry out this creative enterprise, the entrepreneur must have access to the material factors of production, he must be permitted to acquire and trade property. Humans are embodied persons. Our embodiment puts us into a relationship with the material order. The notion of property arises from the relationship that persons maintain with the created order. We leave the imprint of our individuality upon nature by means of the time, effort, and the ability we expend, which, in turn, produces wealth and property. Property rights are really an expression and a safeguard to personal rights. The defense of the right to property, then, ought not be seen as the defense of detached material objects in themselves, but of the dignity, liberty, and the very nature of the human person. The right to property is an extension and exercise of human rights.

The right to work also implies that no one unduly interferes with a person's right to economic participation. This includes the ability to determine one's vocation and type of work. Yet this right of self-determination must be balanced with the concerns and demands of the market. For example, one has the right to determine that one will be an engineer. One does not, however, have the right to demand a

---

7. John Paul II, Encyclical Letter *Laborem Exercens* (September 14, 1981), saluation.

job as an engineer if the market is experiencing an abundance of engineers and cannot accommodate any more. Behind this seeming evil of the free market, however, lies the opportunity for personal ingenuity. To extend the aforementioned example, as the disenchanted engineer searches for a way to support himself physically using his specialized skills, he can "create" his own niche in the world of work. Indeed, the process may be difficult at first, but over time his work will have an effect that transcends the mere gathering of resources. In short, it will express his subjectivity, the unique mingling of his skills and experiences that marks his personhood.

> Work is a good thing for man—a good thing for his humanity—because through work man *not only transforms nature,* adapting it to his own needs, but he also *achieves fulfillment* as a human being and indeed, in a sense, becomes more a human being.[8]

Work is not necessarily a drudgery; rather, it can be seen as a universal part of the human vocation. Indeed, each and every human person is called to an entrepreneurial vocation—a life of productive creativity and self-actualization. This vocation is only fully understood when we consider our obligations to others. The unleashing of human productivity for the sake of the common good is the end result of accepting the call to entrepreneurship of the basic kind—the creative and intelligent use of human resources.

Through creative enterprise the person actualizes both his personhood as well as his potential for service to others. Yet a person must be free to be creative in his work. If his work consists of nothing but mundane tasks with no possibility for creativity, then such work is inconsistent with being a free person. We are referring here to a continuous robotic kind of work that deadens the soul hour after hour. Such work is inhumane because it does not give the worker

8. Ibid., no. 9.3.

the opportunity to be creative, to be virtuous. Such work destroys subjectivity.

Connected to the right to work is the question of opportunity. The modern notion of the right to equal opportunity implies what is often described as "a level playing field," in which no one unjustly inhibits another's chance at employment, housing, education, or social participation. Unfortunately, equal opportunity is often taken to mean equal results.

The right to creative participation does not mean that a person must have the same opportunities as everyone else, for that is impossible. People would have to attain equal human capital and access to the same physical capital for equal opportunity to be a reality. By virtue of differences in family life, social standing, and even genetics, people will necessarily grow up learning different skills. Equal opportunity in the strict sense, therefore, is an impossibility, and does not constitute an essential component of economic liberty. While equal opportunity is not strictly a right, the person does possess a natural immunity from forms of unjust discrimination and oppression that prevent him from full participation in the community.

Creative participation is maximized in a free-market setting. Free markets are the natural social arrangements that arise from human persons exercising their economic liberty. The degree to which all persons are free to participate in the productive sector is the degree to which the market can be considered free.

These reflections lead us to conclude that the primary economic resource is the human person. While natural resources such as water, arable land, and even crude oil are of immense value, they require human intelligence and human labor to be harnessed. As the modern economy develops and technological advances continue, the importance of human expertise and creativity becomes even more apparent. The human race's most valuable asset is itself. We must, therefore, continually strive to find new and constructive ways to educate and train individuals so as to fully maximize human potential. By our choices, initiative, creativity, and investment, we enhance or diminish economic opportunity, community life, and social justice.

WAGE LABOR

When one says *work,* some form of wage employment is what comes to mind immediately in Western industrialized nations. Wage employment is primarily a development and consequence of the industrial revolution of the late 1800s and early 1900s. The emergence of factories and subsequent industries replaced earlier social arrangements of agricultural and guild arrangements. As industrialization spread, more and more people flocked to the cities. Seeking to escape the extreme poverty and hardship of the countryside and taking life in the slums of urban centers as improvements upon the dreadful conditions of the farms, many people entered into wage contracts with those who organized and owned the factories and businesses.

While the history of human work and its surrounding social institutions and forms is fascinating, we are limited in the scope of this paper to discuss primarily wage-labor, the most prevalent form of employment or work in the Western world today. To perform an accurate moral analysis of wage labor we must first understand certain component concepts, such as contract, price, voluntary agreement, mutually beneficial exchange, and the subjectivity of economic value. Those concepts can be best illustrated in an example.

A recent college graduate seeks employment in a given field, hoping to establish a secure and productive career. Managers and employers in that field are frequently in need of skilled, educated labor. Need and circumstance lead to the interview, and if successful, an offer of employment. The offer is in the form of some sort of contract. The contract is expressive of the terms of exchange deemed fair and just by the participants.

The graduate seeks to sell her or his time, skills, strength, intelligence, and activity to another person (the employer) who compensates him or her with money or other material remuneration. One party contracts with the other, each willing to join with the other in an ongoing exchange that is deemed fair and mutually beneficial, yet both subjectively valuing their own property or commodity. A person willingly gives of his or her time and efforts in some creative enterprise in order to provide life's basic necessities from the profit (pay) gained from this expenditure. The effort, energy, and time given by the employee are considered their costs, while the pay package is the benefit or profit. The employer parts with his or her earned cash or resources in order to gain the time, manpower, and resources of the employee.

It is fair to say that the modern concept of work and the workplace has developed in consonance with the twin powerhouses of modernity—industrialization and technological progress. The typical structure of corporate relations is that between owners, managers, and employees. These distinctions are not always descriptively precise, thereby leaving some room for overlap. Needless to say, the normal environs of a workplace can be understood in terms of contracts between employer and employee.

For such a contract to be fair or just, certain elements must be present. First, such an arrangement must be voluntarily entered into by free parties. The terms of the contract must be accepted by both parties freely, with reasonable knowledge of the conditions, terms, and other market factors. The contract, devoid of particulars, usually specifies the type and amount of work to be performed, the condition of the workplace, and the rate of compensation. Ideally, the entire process mutually benefits both parties.

One of the contractual conflicts that may take place is over wages. They are another complicated and controversial aspect of modern employment contracts. Some argue that the prevailing attitude is that the employer should pay *as much as possible* to the employee. Yet the actual meaning of "as much as possible" is difficult to define. It would be better to say that an employer should pay a just wage. Pope Leo XIII used this term:

> A just wage is the legitimate fruit of work. To refuse or withhold it is a serious injustice. In determining fair pay both the needs and contributions of each person must be considered. Mere acknowledgment of the consensual nature to an agreed upon wage between parties is insufficient to justify morally the amount of an employee's salary.[9]

We can summarize these points as follows: In order to be valid and fair, the contract must be consensual, entered into without undue duress, without fraud, and it must be made with regard to the personhood of those involved. Perhaps this last point, "with regard to the personhood of those involved," may be the cause for some consternation among those whose political and social views are libertarian or free-market oriented. The typical argument offered by advocates of a market economy is that any contract entered into freely and honestly is moral. Mutual consent is the only requirement for a contract to be considered just. Yet the addition that the overall working arrangement must also affirm the personhood of those involved seems to muddy the waters at best.

This last addition to the components of a fair contract hearkens back to the words of Pope Leo XIII in his encyclical *Rerum Novarum*. This addition, therefore, is a unique contribution to wage and contract theory made by Christian social teaching. Catholic social teaching affirms the notion of free contractual arrangements.

> Let the working man and the employer make free agreements, and in particular let them agree freely as to the wages; nevertheless, there underlies a dictate of natural justice more imperious and ancient that

9. Leo XIII, Encyclical Letter *Rerum Novarum* (May 15, 1891), no. 45.

any bargain between man and man, namely, that wages ought not to be insufficient to support a frugal and well-behaved wage-earner.[10]

Leo's teaching further elaborated on the morality of the wage contract.

> A just wage is the legitimate fruit of work. To refuse or withhold it can be a grave injustice. In determining fair pay both the needs and the contributions of each person must be taken into account. Remuneration for work should guarantee man the opportunity to provide a dignified livelihood for himself and his family on the material, social, cultural, and spiritual level, taking into account the role and the productivity of each, the state of the business, and the common good.[11]

Just wages, in general, are determined by normal market indicators and rates for comparable work, as well as the free consent of the parties contracting the agreement, usually the employer and the employee. Yet, according to Pope Leo XIII, the idea that wages are *solely* determined by free consent is incomplete. According to Catholic social teaching, labor has two essential characteristics. First, it is personal, inasmuch as the force that acts is bound up with the personality and is the exclusive property of the one who acts. Second, labor is necessary, for without it man cannot live, and self-preservation is a law of nature. Now if work were solely personal, then it would be within the worker's rights to accept any rate of wages whatsoever in the same way he is free to work or not. But our conclusion must be different if we consider the fact that work is also necessary.

Allowing for the worker and the employer to develop a contract includes letting them freely agree upon the wage. Nevertheless, nat-

10. Ibid.
11. Ibid.

ural justice requires that the wages offered should provide for the sustenance of a frugal wage earner.

> If through necessity or fear of a worse evil the worker accepts harder conditions because an employer or contractor will afford him no better, he is made the victim of force and injustice.[12]

While Pope Leo was attempting to develop the church's teaching further, he did not intend to contradict the general tradition's affirmation of the justice of voluntary contracts.

Such an understanding of wages has long been a part of Catholic social teaching. A quick survey of Scholastic thought reveals a predisposition to the market as the primary regulator of wages. Many savants, including Saint Thomas, Saint Bernadino, and Saint Antonino, argued that wages are essentially the "price" of labor.[13] Luis de Molina, from his 1614 treatise, *De Iustitia et Iure,* argued that the best way to gauge the just wage from the market is to examine salaries usually paid for similar jobs in like circumstances:

> After considering the service that an individual undertakes and the large or small number of people who at the same time are found in similar service, if the wage that is set for him is at least the lowest wage that is customarily set in that region at that time for people in such service, the wage is to be considered just.[14]

Another Spanish scholastic, Domingo de Soto, writing before Molina: "[I]f they [workers] freely accepted this salary for their job, it must be just."[15] Franciscan priest Villalobos says that laborers cannot impose their own "justice" on employers.

---

12. *Universal Catechism of the Catholic Church*, nos. 2428–2429.
13. Alejandro A. Chafuen, *Christians For Freedom* (Ignatius Press, 1986), p. 123.
14. Ibid., p. 125.
15. Ibid., p. 126.

And when they [the laborers] say that the wage is below the just minimum, it seems we cannot believe them, because if they could find another [employer] who would pay them more, they would go and work for him, but as they cannot find one, they are like goods that one [the potential buyer] has to beg [to purchase].[16]

Critics of scholastic economics often argue that such views lack adequate compassion, but Chafuen, an expert on scholastic economics, repeatedly emphasizes the savants' awareness that tampering with the market will worsen the worker's condition over time.

The Scholastics were content to allow the market to set wages. Pope Leo, however, appears to find this arrangement lacking. What was Pope Leo after when he pointed out that the demands of justice go beyond mere consensual arrangements? Pope Leo, rather, is seeking to avoid anything that fuels the fire of functionalism.

Functionalization occurs when the individual begins to appear to himself and others as no more than a mere agglomeration of social functions. Instead of viewing the person as a whole, as a mystery, he is reduced to a series of social roles and public tasks that are reductionistic in relation to his overall identity. These functions, while a real facet of man's identity, tend to be taken as the entirety of his identity in certain circles, especially the social sciences. So, rather than man the mystery, we have man the consumer, man the churchgoer, the ticket-collector, the parent, the producer, and so on. The result is that the person and the social order is unnecessarily fragmented.

It should also be noted that the justice of a socioeconomic system and, in each case, its just functioning, deserve in the final analysis to

16. Ibid., p. 127.

be evaluated by the way in which man's work is properly remunerated in the system.[17]

In such a functionalized world the dimension of the mystery of human life is lost. Life is viewed as a series of more or less unrelated functions and problems, rather than a journey or a consistent whole with a unified meaning. Indeed, Gabriel Marcel furthers our understanding of functionalism through his distinction between mystery and problem. While admitting that there are not exact lines of demarcation, Marcel defines a *problem* as a question whose answer, although difficult to obtain, is in theory obtainable. A problem does not fall outside the scope of human intellect. A *mystery*, on the other hand, is a question whose answer will never be fully provided. Mystery goes beyond the ability of the human intellect to fully comprehend. Marcel believes that the person and the things that can be rightly described as personal, are more properly understood as mysteries.

Marcel provides the example of love as a mystery. John and Mary love one another. They think of each other, but they do not, let us suppose, think of love in any abstract way. There is simply the concrete union of mutual love between them. Suppose one of the partners steps back and attempts to analyze what is love? While intelligent thoughts may be made about the subject, and while the subject matter is being experienced by both parties, neither will be able to fully provide an adequate answer to this query.

How does this relate to work? For most in Western culture, functionalization relates closely to occupation. Many people heavily emphasize their professional life when it comes to their overall identity. The answers to the common questions of, Who are you? or, What do you do? are most likely to be in terms of a job—I'm a plumber, or

17. John Paul II, Encyclical Letter *Laborem Exercens* (September 14, 1981), no. 19.

a lawyer, and so on. Admittedly, career plays an important and large role in the lives of many—yet our tendency in industrialized cultures is to give primacy to work.

Accepting this moral truth does not necessitate accepting undue government intrusion in the workplace and contractual agreements, as is often called for in our statist day and age. Nor does this moral fact require enormous and inflated salaries not in accord with market indicators. The Church's advocacy in the affirmation of human dignity in wage contracts is not looking to disregard market principles either. The Church's overall concern is not to denigrate work, but merely to resist any reductionist tendencies. The concern that a just wage contract or employment situation take into consideration the personhood of the employee (and employer for that matter), and not consider merely the monetary aspects to the agreement, is part of this project of defending the overall dignity of the person.

> [A]ccording to natural reason and Christian philosophy, working for gain is creditable, not shameful, to a man, since it enables him to earn an honorable livelihood; but to misuse men as though they were things in the pursuit of gain, or to value them solely for their physical powers—that is truly shameful and inhuman. Again justice demands that, in dealing with the working man, religion and the good of his soul must be kept in mind.[18]

THE ENVIRONMENT OF THE WORKPLACE

Pope John Paul II in *Centesimus Annus* holds a brief discussion on what he terms *human ecology*. By this term the pope means more than standard environmental concerns over natural resources—he is also concerned with the "ecology" of human institutions such as the market and the workplace. The humane treatment of workers is a special concern of the Church. Employers and owners must avoid

---

18. Leo XIII, Encyclical Letter *Rerum Novarum* (May 15, 1891), no. 31.

the temptation to view workers merely in terms of their functions and contributions. Each worker is a person whose dignity and rights must be affirmed and respected. Personalism and Catholic social teaching have reflected on normative dimensions of the workplace and the requirements of a humane ecology regarding the firm, business, or corporation. Several general themes emerge, including the ideas of human capital, participation, and solidarity.

The Church begins its reflections by examining the purpose of a business. The purpose of a business firm is not simply to make a profit. Its purpose is found in its very existence as a community of persons who in various ways satisfy their needs and make a life for themselves. Such a community of persons serves functions that benefit all of society and serve others.[19] Employers and employees, therefore, should join in a concerted effort for their workplace to be a part of the civilization of love spoken of by Pope John Paul II.

> Those *responsible for business enterprises* are responsible to society for the economic and ecological effects of their operations. They have an obligation to consider the good of persons and not merely the increase of *profits*. Profits are necessary, however. They make possible the investments that ensure the future of a business and promote employment.[20]

The Church acknowledges the legitimate role of profit as an indication that a business is functioning well. When a firm makes a profit, this means that the productive factors have been properly employed and corresponding human needs have been duly satisfied. But profitability is not the sole indicator of a firm's health. It is possible for the financial accounts to be in order, and yet for people, who make up the firm's most valuable assets, to have their dignity offended.

Workers are entitled to safe, clean, and humane working condi-

19. John Paul II, Encyclical Letter *Centesimus Annus* (May 1, 1991), no. 35.
20. Ibid.

tions. The work week should be ordered to allow ample time for rest and leisure. Employers are under obligation to provide for the cessation of work on Sundays and certain holy days. Time-off is to be granted for the cultivation of family life, worship, and recreation.[21]

All people possess the right to free association. Workers, therefore, have the right to organize themselves into associations that seek better working conditions and pay. These associations, which should be organized to provide for the betterment of every worker, are bound by the duties of religion and morality.[22] In addition, they are to avoid disharmony at the workplace and are to seek peaceful relations with management. Workers, in turn, have obligations to provide effective service to a company. Workers must exercise temperance, work diligently, and take pride in their craftsmanship.

Leo XIII argues in *Rerum Novarum* that the workplace environment must be taken into account when deciding how long one should work and who should be working. It is unjust, he says, for those working in mines and quarries to work for the same length of time as one working in an office, for example. Children, furthermore, should not work in workshops or factories until their bodies and minds have developed sufficiently.

The type of labor required of the worker also has a moral dimension. Repetitive, monotonous, manual labor that fails to engage the mind and whole personhood of the worker can have devastating personal effects if engaged in for long periods of time. It is impossible, however, for employers to guarantee that employees will derive satisfaction and fulfillment from their work.

These insights of Catholic social teaching, while instructive, require adaptation to specific cultural and economic circumstances. Moral analysis should never occur without the proper consideration of the context of specific circumstances, events, and cultural con-

21. Leo XIII, Encyclical Letter *Rerum Novarum* (May 15, 1891), no. 58.
22. Ibid., no. 69.

ditions. Therefore, Catholic social teaching offers general, normative guidelines that must be prudently applied to varying situations.

In alliance with Christian social teaching, the fundamental concern of affirming the dignity of all persons in all circumstances—the personalist maxim—translates into a myriad of moral goals and aims. One goal rooted in the nature of the personalist maxim is the recognition of the centrality of the human person in economic life. The economy is but the sum-total of individual work. The economy is a result of the totality of free human actions seeking to alleviate the effects of scarcity. The economy originates from human choice. Since all choice contains a moral dimension and the economy necessitates human choice, economic decisions are moral in character.

The human person is at the center of the economy. The Church accepts the methodological individualism that concludes that the market is merely the totality of individual human actions. This leads to the church to conclude that the economy exists for the person, not the person for the economy. It is illegitimate to conceive of the economy as an abstract entity composed of mechanistic aggregates to which society must conform. Economic systems must be in accord with human nature, not the reverse. All economic life should therefore be shaped by how they protect or undermine the life and dignity of the human person—the workplace being no exception.

The above concerns are echoed in the work of personalist philosophers and theologians of the twentieth century. Many personalist authors resisted the notion of functionalism (spoken of earlier) in their work. They understood that work contained an instrumental character to it that is served as some means to an end. Yet it was important for the employer and all those involved in the enterprise not ever to conceive of the person who supplies the labor as a means to an end. Persons, to take the positive side of Kant's dictum, must always be viewed as ends in themselves, never as means to a greater end.

This framework, clearly, does not rule out a proper understanding of the instrumentality of work and even, in a limited sense, of the person who provides it. Yet understanding the instrumental character of work is not the same thing as harboring a functionalist attitude. The value attributed to the person, according to a functionalist mentality, is equivalent with his or her output or social or economic utility. Now, of course, we are not saying that pay must be equal, or that the economic value ascribed to human work must be seen as equal. That would be not only ridiculous, but also economically disastrous.

The greatest economic and moral asset of any company or business is the people who comprise it.

> In our time, in particular, there exists another form of ownership which is becoming no less important than land: the possession of know-how, technology, and skill. The wealth of industrialized nations is based more on this kind of ownership than on natural resources.[23]

This reality allows us to speak of human capital. We introduce this notion not to reinforce any economic or functionalist notions but rather to enhance the understanding of the value and centrality of the human person to all of social life, the economy and business sectors not withstanding.

Capital is best defined as anything that can be used as a means of production. There are five primary types of capital: *natural capital* (including land and natural resources), *man-made capital* (produced means of production), *physical human capital* (manual labor), *intellectual capital* (creativity, intelligence), and *interpersonal capital* (an individual's relationships that help him to produce things he could not by himself).

Capital is literally instrumental to human action. It is a tool, not an end in itself, and the creation or accumulation of capital is always for some other purpose. The acting person requires capital in order

23. John Paul II, Encyclical Letter *Centesimus Annus* (May 1, 1991), no. 32.

to exercise freedom effectively and obtain even the most meager standard of living. The concept of capital and capital formation serves to underscore the economic centrality of the acting person.

> Many goods cannot be adequately produced through the work of an isolated individual; they require the cooperation of many people in working towards a common goal. Organizing such a productive effort, planning its duration in time, making sure that it corresponds in a positive way to the demands which it must satisfy, and taking the necessary risks—all this too is a source of wealth in today's society. In this way, the role of disciplined and creative human work and, as an essential part of that work, initiative and entrepreneurial ability becomes increasingly evident and decisive. This process, which throws practical light on a truth about the person which Christianity has constantly affirmed, should be viewed carefully and favorably. Indeed, besides the earth, man's principal resource is man himself.[24]

Capital is any resource, whether natural or human, that may be employed productively. There is a close link between capital and creativity. Because all human action has a creative aspect, action is constantly creating new goods, services, and insights. As needs become known, new opportunities arise for creative action. In this respect, the human condition is constantly shifting; we never fully know what needs will exist in the future nor how those needs will be met. Hence, the primary form of capital—human capital—is our ability to respond creatively to needs as they arise. Because all goods and institutions produced or designed by human beings ultimately derive value from the human capital upon which they rest, they must foster the development of that capital if they are to be effective in the future.

Human capital may be accumulated. While all persons have the potential for creativity, and indeed exercise it through their actions,

24. Ibid.

individual persons possess varying degrees of human capital. Some persons develop their intelligence, industry, and creativity in a way that enables them to foresee needs and work productively. This development accumulates human capital. It is important to note that those who store more capital than others do not somehow maintain greater dignity than those who have not. People who invest their capital through entrepreneurial activity, however, deserve the greater material rewards that they earn. To deny such rewards is an offense against the value of human creativity, and thus against the dignity of the human person.

The full meaning of human capital cannot be understood until we have a clear idea of the nature of property, because capital presupposes property. Those things considered to be capital, if not owned by the person seeking to utilize them, cannot be properly used to invest where it is most productive. It is the right of the one who owns the capital only to utilize the capital, when he has not, justly and fairly, contracted it out. The idea of human capital as a person's intelligence, industry, and creativity, in fact, necessarily implies that a person has the power to follow his judgment as to when, how, and for what value he should act. Without the freedom to dispose of one's possessions in order to satisfy a need creatively, human capital loses its foundation in creativity. Hence, human capital requires property, which, put simply, is everything a person owns.

The application of human capital can be described broadly as entrepreneurial. The prudent person finds ways to maximize his potential and, thus, adequately meet his needs and the needs of others. Since each person possesses human capital and to some degree develops that capital, it is fair to refer to the universal vocation of entrepreneurship, which is obviously linked to business and market activity. A vocation such as that is often held in moral suspicion by Christians.

Asserting an entrepreneurial vocation takes into consideration that all people have the right to economic initiative, to productive work, to just wages and benefits, to decent working conditions, and to free association in the productive aspects of the social order. These conditions and rights can be summed up in one word—participation. Participation should be the normal situation of all members of society. Participaqtion is the person acting in communion with others. Involvement in social groups results in the benefit of affirmation of self and thus is necessary for human flourishing.[25]

Participation is not merely a general goal for society and social institutions, yielding a benefit, but also a goal of the workplace. Meaningful employment is one of the primary means of social involvement in mainstream Western society. In an industrialized economy, maintaining a job is the normal way for individuals and families to participate in the productive sector of society. Through such participation, workers satisfy their needs and contribute to the common good.

The common good necessitates that everyone has a right to participate in the productive sphere. This does not mean that everyone has a right to a particular job or form of employment; rather, it implies that people should make legitimate use of their talents in such a way that will benefit everyone else. Regarding access to employment, there should be no unjust discrimination between men and women, healthy and disabled, natives and immigrants.[26]

Besides unjust discrimination, participation at the workplace translates into two central concerns. First, when possible, workers should have reasonable autonomy and decision-making ability regarding their own positions and tasks. Second, the worker must respect the owner's authority and autonomy to operate his or her industry or organization, based upon the employer upholding his or

25. Emmanuel Mounier, *Personalism* (Notre Dame: University of Notre Dame Press, 1952), p. 21.
26. *Universal Catechism of the Catholic Church*, no. 2433.

her obligation to maintain a workplace ecology that affirms the human dignity of each individual whom he or she employs.

The worker should be encouraged to take initiative and demonstrate responsible stewardship over his or her tasks—this includes being granted autonomy so that he or she may establish an advantageous self-direction. The worker, thus granted this degree of self-direction, will participate more fully in the overall life and direction of the company. Restated in business terminology, participation means avoiding the micromanaging of employees. People, when possible, should be afforded the highest degree of self-discretion and self-direction as possible and not viewed merely in terms of their social utility or performance of specific tasks. Promoting participation at the workplace thus respects human dignity and creativity and can lead to improved morale and productivity at the office.

Second, participation at the workplace also implies a respect for the autonomy and authority of the management by workers. If a company is to flourish, not only must the worker be given the respect that is due him or her, but management must also be given a reciprocal respect. Management, because of their more intimate contact with the employee, has a solid understanding of that worker's needs—including safety, health, financial, and spiritual—more than any external source. This level of understanding enhances the morale of the workplace, therefore increasing productivity and efficiency. When management affords the workers with the dignity and respect each is due, and they reciprocate in kind, a bond of solidarity further enhances the morale of the workplace.

This bond of solidarity is often understood as a fundamental moral measure of any economy, most recognized in its relation to how the poor and vulnerable are faring. This is because society has a moral obligation to assure opportunity, meet basic human needs, and pursue justice in economic life. Christian social thought has always taught, echoing the Gospel, that Christians have a moral obligation to help the poor. The exact nature of that help needs to be discerned in light of the specific circumstances of the given people in need. Cultivating an attitude of solidarity that seeks social justice, however, is not an option but a requirement of all followers of Christ. Emmanuel Mounier argues that true solidarity has the ability "to sustain, together with others, a society of persons, the structure, the customs, the sentiments and the institutions of which are shaped by their nature as persons."[27]

Solidarity needs be practiced not only in our associations among neighbors and the poor, but also among fellow workers at all employment levels; from the newly employed to the owner, each must have solidarity with the other. A company or business is comprised of the individuals who hold a share in it, work for it, or contribute to its overall success and functioning. Each of these individuals has his or her own set of interests, and each is united together in their common goal of the success and thriving of the company. Therefore, solidarity is a necessary part of the workplace environment. Recognized by most companies today, the creation of solidarity has taken a larger role in their operations, utilizing the participatory and creative nature of the individuals. Rope courses, retreats, and team meetings are ways in which this calling is put into action.

The call of solidarity and participation in the workplace are vehicles toward the recognition of human dignity and personhood.

> But here it must be emphasized, in general terms, that the person who works desires *not only* due *remuneration* for his work; he also wishes that, within the production process, provision be made for him to be able to *know* that in his work, even on something that is owned in common, he is working *"for himself."*[28]

Solidarity and effective participation not only will result in an understanding of place in the production process, but also positively affects

27. Mounier, p. 21.
28. Robert A. Sirico, *Economics, Faith and Moral Responsibility*, p. 12.

the entire life of workers. Thus, these principles resulting from the needs of the common good effect that set of social conditions in which individuals and groups of individuals flourish and meet their proper ends.

CONCLUDING REMARKS

Human work proceeds directly from persons created in God's image who have been called to subdue the earth. In work, people exercise and fulfill some of the creative potential inscribed in their nature. The central value of work stems from the person, as its author and beneficiary.

We must acknowledge that work exists for persons, not persons for work.[29] Work is not part of the curse God cast on humankind as the penalty for sin. The curse promised *hardship* in multiplying (Gen. 3:16) and in subduing the earth (Gen. 17–19). That humans should work as part of their expression of the Creator's image was ordained prior to the Fall (Gen. 1:26–28; 2:15, 18).[30] Thus, work is a privilege. The inverse of work, sloth, is condemned not only as rebellion against God's immediate command, but also as a dehumanizing repression of God's image.[31]

A person's talents are as much his or her own as his or her life; the possibility of using them for his or her own personal good and for the common good is a prerequisite in the development of personality. The realization of this right depends on proportionately equal educational facilities and upon a market economy that makes the choice of employment possible. The regimentation of labor in a centrally planned economy, especially any kind of forced labor, clashes with this right, except in extreme cases of national emergency.

29. John Paul II, Encyclical Letter *Laborem Exercens* (September 14, 1981), nos. 12–15.
30. Beisner, p. 30.
31. Messner, p. 329.

With the importance of work in mind, we must not lose sight that unemployment is a grave social ill. Long-term unemployment always wounds the dignity of its victims and threatens the equilibrium of their lives. Besides personal harm done to individuals, it entails many risks for the families of workers.[32]

Christian entrepreneurs are called to employ their God-given talents to the fullest extent possible in service to others, including opportunities for meaningful employment. What implication does this call have upon those in the vocation of business? It means that they must strive to display more fully the virtue of inventiveness, to act more boldly with the virtue of creativity, and to continue to be other-regarding as they anticipate market demands. While they educate others in the virtue of thrift, they should not merely distribute resources to those in need, but teach them how to produce wealth for themselves independently.

The capacities of each human person for love, creativity, reasoned acquisition of material resources, generosity, and charity bespeak the notion of human capital. Each of us are called to apply human capital for our own sake and the well-being of others. This application, of course, will take on many forms as entrepreneurs enter the marketplace to serve their neighbor through the production of goods and services. The call to business activity—to entrepreneurship—should not be held in moral suspicion. All people have the right to make a livelihood, that is, to secure the necessities of life by work. While any vocation may be motivated by greed or the pursuit of selfish gain, not everyone suffers from such base motivations.

Christ's redeeming love in the Incarnation sanctifies the created order and attests to the dignity of man. The call to a life of dignity brings with it the expectation that we will share in the traits of our Creator and Father, namely, that we will use our love, intellect, and will to create for ourselves, others, and the glory of God.

32. *Universal Catechism of the Catholic Church*, no. 2436.

CHAPTER THREE

Mandating Employee Benefits: Harming Workers and Undermining the Morality of the Labor Market

Dwight R. Lee
Richard B. McKenzie

A FREE LABOR MARKET is a force for the well-being of workers and an important contributor to the freedom and responsibility upon which human flourishing depends. The pure economic advantage of labor markets—by which we mean the unfettered buying and selling of workers' skills and efforts—is found in their ability to disseminate various forms of information on the relative social value (at the margin) of alternative employment opportunities and to motivate employers and employees to respond appropriately to the information. When wages and salaries are determined by mutual agreement between employees and employers, the general efficiencies that result benefit all workers, not only by creating opportunities for them to best utilize their productive talents, but also by creating an environment in which they make wise choices as consumers and investors. But more importantly, free labor markets contribute to the social order that depends on, and fosters, individual freedom. The morality of the labor market, as does the morality of markets in general, derives from the discipline it imposes, thereby insuring that freedom will be exercised responsibly. Only when freedom is exercised responsibly will a full measure of freedom be tolerated. And freedom will be exercised responsibly only when the best way to seek personal objectives is by responding to the concerns and circumstances of others, as communicated through market prices.

Unfortunately the benefits from the efficient allocation of labor and from freedom are general benefits that are easily taken for granted and difficult to trace back to the discipline of labor markets. And because of the general nature of the benefits, no one individual (or organized groups of individuals) is motivated to understand their source or contribute to their maintenance. On the other hand, the discipline imposed by free labor markets is readily seen as an inconvenience by those subjected to it, and they can easily identify the source of that inconvenience—the competition allowed by free labor markets. This bias in the perception of the costs and benefits of free labor markets has led to political pressures in favor of a host of government restrictions on those markets.

In this chapter we shall consider the effect of labor market restrictions in the form of government mandates that employers provide additional compensation to their employees, either with higher wages (minimum-wage legislation) or by providing them with nonmonetary benefits (fringe benefits). While the advantages to workers from these mandated benefits may seem obvious, the sad reality is that they directly harm the very workers who are supposedly helped. Furthermore, by distorting the operation of labor markets, mandated benefits indirectly harm us all by undermining the responsibility and freedom, and thus the morality, of social interaction.

THE LABOR MARKET AS A PROCESS

Do workers receive fair compensation for their effort? This is an impossible question to answer with any hope of agreement if we attempt to answer it by concentrating on particular outcomes. How much compensation in the form of wages and fringe benefits should any particular worker, or occupational group, receive? The problem lies in the host of considerations that affect workers' evaluation of various types of employment, not the least of which are the work demands, the conditions inside the workplace, the environment (weather and distance from homes) surrounding the workplace, the prospects for future advancement and higher incomes, and the attitudes and abilities of coworkers. For example, one worker in one firm in one location might be less highly compensated in terms of wages and fringes than someone else in another firm in another location simply because of more work-based amenities or a higher probability of being paid more in the future. Moreover, workers differ in how they evaluate the various factors of employment. Some workers may care little about long commutes to work, while others consider long commutes a serious problem.

There is no sensible way of considering the question of the fairness of compensation outside the context of the process that generates the compensation. The best we can do is to compare alternative processes for determining compensation, and evaluate them on the basis of how well they serve the general interests of those affected. Such an evaluation has to recognize that no realistic alternative can overcome scarcity (or the physical limits on what workers can do for employers and what employers can do for workers in return). Therefore, the best possible process will generate outcomes, which completely satisfy no one. Much of this chapter will be a comparison of two broad processes for determining employee compensation, the market process and the political process. Additional alternatives could be considered by comparing variations of the market and political processes, but little, if anything, would be gained from the additional effort. The discussion will make clear that market processes tend to dominate political processes at generating a pattern of outcomes that benefit the general public, particularly employees.[1]

1. We assume that there are no significant distributional differences between

The advantage that employees realize from the market process is rooted in the freedom allowed them because of the discipline imposed in the labor market. In a properly functioning labor market, no one can require that an employer hire particular workers. The only way workers can get jobs is by their holding out the prospects of providing high enough value, or accepting low enough compensation, to make their employment profitable to their employers. If a worker decides not to be very productive, as determined by others, because (for example) he values the easy life, he suffers a loss in terms of lower compensation. Therefore, "society" has little stake in the decision any particular person makes on how productive to be, certainly far less stake than if workers were given a claim on some level of income independent of their productivity. Labor markets impose enough discipline on workers to permit "society" to tolerate a great deal of freedom on the part of workers to be more or less productive, as they choose.

Because of the freedom in free labor markets, no employer can require anyone to work. The only way an employer can secure the services of a worker is by paying enough to attract the worker away from the most valuable alternative use of the worker's time, whether that use is some alternative employment or a leisure-time activity. So workers can be assured of receiving compensation that covers their opportunity costs as determined by their preferences and the decisions they make regarding their training and effort. This freedom of workers, coupled with the freedom of consumers to buy or not buy what firms produce, also impose a stout discipline on employers. They have to pay enough to attract competent workers while keeping

---

the market process and the political process we describe. Those who believe that an advantage of the political process over the marketplace is that the former generates more equal outcomes will object to this assumption. But, as we have argued elsewhere (Lee and McKenzie, 1988), competition exists no matter what the process, and there is no reason to believe that political competition leads to more equal outcomes than does market competition.

costs low enough to keep the price of their products attractive to consumers. In effect, employers are constrained by the competition of other employers for workers and the competition of other producers for consumer dollars.

This market-based discipline allows freedom and, at the same time, enhances the freedom it allows. This freedom, and the opportunities it creates for people to improve their lives as they see fit in productive cooperation with others, are the primary advantages of labor markets. It should also be clear why the discipline of labor markets serves the interest of people so well in their roles as workers and consumers. First, there is the competitive pressure on employers to pay workers at least what their aptitude and skills make them worth elsewhere in the economy. This ensures that workers receive full benefit from their efforts to improve their productivity. Second, quite apart from their own efforts, the productivity of workers is constantly being increased by the investments that employers make in capital, equipment, and innovations to meet the ongoing competition for consumer patronage.

Of course, workers are in competition with other workers for jobs, and employers take advantage of that competition to keep the cost of employee compensation as low as possible. But this explains the third advantage workers, in their role as consumers, receive from labor markets. The competitive pressure employers face to keep costs and the price of their products low increases the value of the compensation that workers receive.

The discipline imposed by labor markets also explains why employers not only provide fringe benefits, but also why they provide that mix of fringe benefits and monetary compensation that best serves the interest of employees without government mandates. By considering the economics of fringe benefits in more detail we will be able to consider better the harm done by government-inspired labor-market mandates.

WHY EMPLOYERS PROVIDE FRINGE BENEFITS

It is clear that employers do not require government mandates to get them to provide their workers with fringe benefits. Such benefits are widely provided. At first glance the existence of fringe benefits might seem difficult to explain. Why don't firms eliminate fringe benefits and use the cost savings to increase their employee's salaries and wages? This would allow employees to buy what they want instead of what their employers decide to provide. The answer is that there are some things that employees value that can only be provided by employers or that can be provided more cheaply by employers. Safer working conditions, annual leave, flexible working hours, and on-the-job training are examples of employee benefits that only employers can provide. Freshly laundered uniforms, meals in a fast-food establishment, certain types of training, and health insurance are examples of benefits employees can purchase elsewhere but which can generally be provided at lower cost by their employer. Obviously, there are gains to be had by both employees and employers from employers providing such fringe benefits.

But what combination of money payments and fringes should employers provide? Answering this question takes us right back to the competition in free labor markets as the most dependable force for achieving efficient monetary and fringe benefit mixes in compensation packages. As discussed earlier, competition among firms for consumer dollars requires that they keep their costs, including labor costs, as low as possible while securing an adequate number of competent and motivated workers. But competition among firms for workers requires employers to obtain those workers by offering them combinations of money payments and fringes that are at least as attractive, and preferably more attractive, than those of other firms. Providing fringe benefits is an effective way for firms to increase the value of their compensation packages to workers while holding down their labor costs. This explains why firms are constantly on the lookout for fringe benefits that are worth more to their workers than the fringes cost.

A simple example may be helpful in understanding how fringes can control firms' employment costs. Assume that a firm can provide each employee with health insurance at a cost of $300 per month, which is less than employees would have to pay for individual coverage, which we assume is worth $400 per month to each of them.

The firm will surely provide the health insurance since, by doing so, it can simultaneously reduce its labor costs and pay its workers more. For example, by providing the insurance, the firm can reduce the monetary pay to each worker by, say, $350 per month, which reduces its labor costs per worker by $50 per month, while increasing the total value of the compensation package to each worker by $50 per month.[2]

Our example actually understates the motivation firms have to supply their employees with fringe benefits. Each firm has to fear that other firms will provide the fringe benefit (health insurance), hire away workers, and, because the other firms have lower labor costs, be able to offer their products at lower prices.

Moreover, because employees are taxed on monetary wages but not on the value of most fringe benefits, there are private gains to be shared between a firm and its employees in providing fringe benefits that have a social value less than their social cost. Hence, firms may provide benefits that shouldn't be provided at all, and will invariably provide benefits beyond the point where the marginal value and cost of the fringe provided are equal.

To see this point, assume that reducing the deductibility required on health care insurance by $1,000 is worth $20 per month to each

---

2. There is no reason to expect that the total gain will be split evenly between employer and employees. Depending on the relative elasticities of demand for and supply of labor, most of the gain can go to the employer or the employees. But with the exception of extreme cases (infinitely elastic supply of labor, or zero elasticity in the demand for labor), both employer and employees will share in the gains.

employee, but costs the firm an additional $25 per month for each employee. Obviously, this upgrade in health care coverage is not warranted. But if the marginal income tax faced by each worker is, say, 33 percent, the nontaxable upgrade in the deductible is worth just under $30 in taxable income. Thus, the company will provide the upgrade and reduce monthly salaries by somewhere between $25 and $30, leaving both the firm and its workers better off by adding a socially wasteful fringe benefit. Given this tax distortion, there is little reason for concern that employers will fail to provide fringe benefits to their employees that are worth more than they cost.

So far we have simplified the discussion by assuming that all employees in a firm place the same value on each fringe benefit. Obviously, this is not true. Workers typically value fringe benefits differently. Older workers with families, for example, will generally place a high value on health insurance. On the other hand, young workers, who tend to use less medical care and, anyway, are likely covered by their parent's health insurance, will see little value in having their own health care coverage (especially if the cost of health insurance is significantly inflated by the presence of older workers who make use of it). Rather than health insurance, younger workers are more likely to prefer a combination of higher wages and more flexible working hours to accommodate, perhaps, their class schedules. The better a firm can accommodate such diverse preferences, the better able it is to attract good workers for a given cost, which explains why firms commonly provide a menu of fringe benefits from which its employees can choose.

Of course, even with a menu of fringe benefits, it is difficult for an employer to tailor fringe benefits perfectly to the preferences of all workers. Depending on the size of the firm, the type of skills it requires, its location, and many other considerations, different firms will face different costs of providing a given mix of fringe benefits. So the most cost-effective fringe benefit packages being offered will vary over firms, with workers able to self-select into those firms that provide the combination of fringe benefit and monetary compensation that best suits their situations.[3]

This may mean that some worker groups will receive some benefits—for example health insurance or subsidized education—that are not received by other worker groups. But this does not mean that either worker group is "worse off" because some fringe is not received. Indeed, the opposite is likely to be the case. Young workers may get less in the way of health insurance but more money wages (with the additional money wages expected to be greater than the value of the health insurance foregone). Older workers, on the other hand, may get less in money wages (than they would otherwise) but more in the way of health insurance (that would have cost the older workers more to buy individually than collectively through their employers via lower wages).

The ability of the workers to sort themselves by their desired combinations of money wages and fringe benefits ensures that the fringes are used with constraint—that is, responsibly. If workers were not able to sort themselves by their need for, say, health insurance, then (older) workers could anticipate that a portion of the cost of their health care could be transferred to other (younger) workers, thus reducing the perceived cost of health care with an expected increase in the use of health care (for purposes the value of which are not worth their full cost), and a concomitant increase in the cost of health insurance and a reduction in worker wages. The ability of workers to sort themselves among employers thereby holds workers wages (and the total value of their compensation packages) higher than they would otherwise be.

---

3. For example, Long and Marquis (1992) find similar demographic characteristics among workers who do not take health insurance coverage when their firms offer it as an option, and those workers in firms that do not offer health insurance.

HARMING WORKERS WITH MANDATED BENEFITS

It should now be clear why employers provide fringe benefits to their employees. It pays them to do so! There are several important conclusions to be drawn from our discussion that leads to this conclusion.

First, despite the statements of politicians suggesting that they are providing workers with a free lunch with governmentally mandated benefits, employers do not "give" their workers fringe benefits, whether mandated or otherwise. Employees "pay" for fringe benefits with wage reductions (or with smaller wage increases than they would otherwise receive). In effect, firms "sell" their workers fringe benefits. They typically sell them for more than they cost the firm to provide, but for less than the workers value them—which means that both sides benefit from the implied trades. But the fringes are not a free lunch for workers, and nothing politicians are able to do can change that fact.

Second, employers are in the best position to know the costs of providing fringe benefits and their value to their workers. Furthermore, employers have a stronger motivation to use that information appropriately than does anyone else. When an employer makes a mistake by providing a fringe benefit that is worth less than it costs, the employer receives feedback in terms of workers moving to other producers and/or in terms of customers moving to producers who have not made the same mistake and, therefore, can charge lower prices. The employer suffers the losses from mistakes and reaps the gains from avoiding or correcting them.

The adjustment process that competitive forces encourage is not without flaws, because people are not without flaws in the way they can and are willing to adjust. Some mistakes in compensation packages might endure. However, the relevant issue is whether any other method of adjusting compensation packages to accommodate worker and employer (and consumer) preferences is likely to make fewer mistakes. Certainly employers are more likely to choose cost-effective fringe benefits than are political decision makers. Politicians and bureaucrats, who are not involved directly in the firms who are paying the workers and who are in far-removed state and national capitals, cannot possibly have the information necessary to improve upon the compensation plans of all firms in their jurisdictions, and adjust those plans in response to changing local conditions. This is true even in small jurisdictions. Politicians and bureaucrats simply aren't "there," and have no way of knowing the relative costs of various benefits and the various preferences of different worker groups in the different industries within any given governmental jurisdiction. Who can seriously believe that federal officials are knowledgeable enough to improve upon the compensation plans of all firms in the entire economy? Furthermore, even if government officials did somehow have as much information relevant to each firm's compensation as does each firm, their motivation to make appropriate use of the information is necessarily impaired, given that a portion of the costs of mistakes can be transferred to the workers and employers. The politicians and bureaucrats would realize less gain than the workers and employers from utilizing the available information wisely, and would suffer less in the way of losses if they used their information unwisely. Indeed, there are good reasons for believing that the politicians and bureaucrats have incentives to misuse the information at their disposal. The political power to mandate employee benefits is a power that attracts organized interest groups. These groups will reward politicians for imposing uniform mandates (guaranteed not to be appropriate for all employers) for the purpose of reducing the competition they (the organized interests) face from other employees and other firms.[4]

4. For example, union member workers tend to be older and value health insurance more than do younger workers. Therefore, unionized firms typically provide such insurance as a fringe benefit. Other firms, smaller and nonunionized, operating in the same industry, can more effectively compete against the unionized firms by hiring younger workers without providing them the health insurance they

Third, because of the lack of relevant information and perverse incentives in the political process, when fringe benefits are mandated, they are likely to harm workers. Mandating a fringe benefit requires providing something to workers that costs them more than it is worth—otherwise it would have already been provided. (Employers will gladly provide any benefit the value of which to workers exceeds the costs to the employer, simply because that would mean the employer can increase its profits.) At least some of the costs of the fringe benefits to workers will be felt by workers, as discussed earlier, in the form of sacrificed money income that they, the workers, would otherwise have earned. But mandated fringe benefits also necessarily crowd out other benefits that employees value more than those that are mandated. For example, a young college student will probably value flexible working hours, with opportunities to take some unpaid leave occasionally, far more than he or she values health insurance. But if an employer has to provide health insurance to all employees, a cost that is independent of the hours worked, flexible hours and time off are unlikely to be provided. So, mandates restrict the ability of firms to offer their workers a menu of fringe benefits that best suit their individual situations. And federal mandates, by imposing such restrictions uniformly over the entire country, reduce the ability of workers to find and take advantage of differences in fringe benefit packages among firms to obtain that compensation mix that maximizes the value they realize from their jobs. Such benefits necessarily lower the benefits workers can realize by sorting themselves among firms, once again adding to the uncompensated net cost of the mandates.

---

don't value as much as it costs. Clearly it is in the interest of the unionized firms, and their unions, to have the government mandate that all firms provide health insurance to their workers. For an extension of this explanation for union support of mandated benefits, see Lee (1997).

Obviously, many workers are harmed on balance by mandated benefits. Having the government require employers to provide certain benefits to their workers (or specify the characteristics of the benefits that employers choose to provide) replaces the flexibility of the marketplace to respond to local information with the rigidities and the one-size-fits-all mentality of central planning. While mandates are directed at employers, they also tell workers what to do, and these directions are given by remote authorities who believe they know best what workers should have (a belief commonly shared and encouraged by influential special-interest groups). Workers would surely protest strenuously if a law were passed that required that they all had to buy expensive books of poetry every month or purchase organically-grown health food. The problem with such a mandate is not that poetry and health food aren't desirable, but that most people don't value them by as much as they cost.[5] The same unfavorable cost-benefit ratios are true for mandated employee benefits. But employees are docile when these benefits are mandated partly because they have been convinced that employers pay for them (and might be temporarily paid less by employers until they have time to adjust the compensation mix). But the harm to workers from mandated benefits is no less real because it is disguised and delayed.

5. We recognize that employee preferences for employer-provided benefits cannot be catered to with quite the same individuality as can books of poetry or health food. But there is more independence of choice than most realize because of the opportunity to select among different employers and because of the employers' desire to cater to individual employee preferences by providing menus of fringe benefits. Certainly the choices are more varied when employee benefits are not mandated than when they are. One can argue that by requiring everyone (all employees) to pay for a fringe benefit, it is cheaper for everyone. That may be true, but it would also be true of books of poetry and organic foods. Also, employers, when deciding on the mix of money and fringe benefits in their compensation packages, take such economies of scale into consideration.

THE MINIMUM WAGE AS A MANDATED BENEFIT

The harm mandated benefits impose on workers applies with full force to the minimum wage. Indeed the minimum wage is best thought of as a mandated benefit, albeit one that is taxed. And, as is the case with mandating any employee benefit, mandating an increase in the wage some workers are paid harms those workers by requiring that they pay more for the benefit than it is worth to them. In the case of conventional mandated benefits, workers pay for them with sacrificed monetary compensation. In the case of a minimum-wage hike, workers who receive an increase in their mandated wage (we assume here that they keep their jobs) pay for that increase with sacrificed fringe benefits.

Those who favor minimum-wage legislation (or mandated benefits in general) view the world as does Adam Smith's (1982, p. 234) "man of system [who] seems to imagine that he can arrange the different members of a great society with as much ease as the hand arranges the different pieces on a chessboard. He does not consider that the pieces upon a chessboard have no other principle of motion besides that which the hand impresses upon them; but that, in the great chessboard of human society, every single piece has a principle of motion of its own, altogether different from that which the legislature might choose to impress upon it." Employers and employees have their own principles of motion, and they respond to minimum-wage hikes in ways that their advocates have failed to see, or refuse to acknowledge.

Employers respond to an increase in the minimum wage in a number of ways. The employer response opponents of the minimum wage mention the most (indeed, almost exclusively) is dismissing low-skilled workers, or never hiring them in the first place, since the value of their marginal product is less than the mandated wage. This response obviously harms low-skilled workers by denying them opportunities, but it is not the only, or necessarily the most harmful, response of employers to minimum-wage increases.

Requiring that employers pay certain workers a higher wage is not the same as requiring that they increase their compensation. Employers can, and do, respond to increases in the minimum wage by reducing nonmonetary benefits to the workers who now receive more money. Other possible ways employers can respond are numerous. Fast-food workers may no longer be provided uniforms or laundry service, a charge for meals may be imposed, assignments that incorporate a large measure of on-the-job training may be replaced with more routine and repetitious tasks, choices allowed in working hours may be reduced, and/or more work per hour may be required (or less slack time may be allowed)—just to mention a few of the possible adjustments made in response to a minimum-wage hike. These benefits may not be lost immediately (and the loss may take the form of not providing new benefits that would otherwise have been provided), but as long as the employer's cost of the fringe benefits provided (or soon to be provided) are at least equal to the increase in the minimum wage, expect that cost to be reduced as the required wage cost is increased.

And make no mistake about it, a minimum-wage hike gives employers the ability to dictate reductions in fringe benefits or increases in work demands. This is because, without the adjustments, the minimum-wage hike destroys the net profitability of some jobs and, at the same time, increases the number of workers who are willing to work in the areas covered by the minimum wage. The resulting increases in the market surpluses of labor permit employers to curb benefits or impose greater work demands and, in effect, say to workers, "Take it or leave it." Moreover, competition is not obliterated by the minimum-wage hike. Employers must make adjustments in fringes and work demands just to hold their costs and prices in line with those of competitors.

Because the cost of employing most minimum-wage workers will not be increased by the same amount as the increases in the minimum wage (because fringe benefits are reduced or work demands are increased), employers will not lay off (or refuse to hire) as many workers as might be expected if only the wage cost of hiring labor is considered. This may provide a partial explanation for why some empirical studies have found increases in the minimum wage have a small, if not inconsequential, impact of teenage employment.[6]

However, we stress that it is not just employers who respond to the minimum wage. The employer response, or demand-side response, is the one that discussions of the minimum wages focus on almost entirely, but it ignores the equally important worker, or supply-side, response.

Consider the effect on workers of the adjustments employers make to increases in the minimum wage, and their response to the adjustments. If the extra money from a minimum-wage increase was worth more to workers than the benefits lost, employers would have reduced labor costs and would, accordingly, be able to attract better workers by making the substitution without a hike in the wage being mandated. The fact that employers don't boost their wages is strong evidence that an increase in the minimum wage harms even those workers who keep their jobs.[7] In other words, even though employers

---

6. Another explanation might be flaws in the studies claiming little if any unemployment effect. However, considering the controversies that surround such studies, any further exploration on our part here would take us beyond the scope of this chapter.

7. Writing in the *American Economic Review*, Masanori Hashimoto found that under the 1967 minimum-wage hike, workers gained thirty-two cents in money income but lost forty-one cents per hour in training—a net loss of nine cents an hour in full-income compensation (Hashimoto, 1982). Linda Leighton and Jacob Mincer (1981), in one study, and Belton Fleisher (1981), in another study, came to a similar conclusion: increases in the minimum wage reduce on-the-job training—and, as a result, dampen growth in the real long-run income of covered workers. Walter Wessels (1987) found that the minimum wages caused retail establishments in New York to increase work demands. In response to a minimum-wage increase, only 714 of the surveyed stores cut back store hours, but 4,827 stores reduced the number of workers and/or their employees' hours worked. Thus, in most stores,

are spending as much (maybe a little more) on employee compensation after a minimum-wage increase than before, that compensation is worth less to workers. Since workers have their own principles of motion, because they find minimum-wage jobs less attractive after the minimum wage is increased, they will find other alternatives, such as leisure, welfare, and crime, relatively more attractive. While having more people choose these alternatives to working is unfortunate, both for the individual and the broader community, the reduction in people looking for work has the effect of taking them out of the official unemployment statistics.

Again, the harmful effects of the minimum wage motivate workers to respond in ways that explain why many studies fail to find much unemployment caused by minimum-wage increases. The unemployment caused by increasing the minimum wage is a woefully incom-

---

fewer workers were given fewer hours to do the same work as before. The research of Belton Fleisher (1981), William Alpert (1983), and L. F. Dunn (1985) shows that minimum-wage increases lead to large reductions in fringe benefits and to worsening working conditions. If the minimum wage does *not* cause employers to make substantial reductions in nonmoney benefits, then increases in the minimum wage should cause (1) an increase in the labor-force participation rates of covered workers (because workers would be moving up their supply-of-labor curves), (2) a reduction in the rate at which covered workers quit their jobs (because their jobs would then be more attractive), and (3) a significant increase in prices of production processes heavily dependent on covered minimum-wage workers. However, Wessels (1987) found little empirical support for such conclusions drawn from conventional theory. Indeed, in general, he found that minimum-wage increases had the exact opposite effect: (1) participation rates went down, (2) quit rates went up, and (3) prices did not rise appreciably—findings consistent only with the view that minimum-wage increases make workers worse off. With regard to quit rates, Wessels (1987, p. 13) writes,

I could find no industry which had a significant decrease in their quit rates. Two industries had a significant increase in their quit rates. . . . These results are only consistent with a lower full compensation. I also found that quit rates went up more in those industries with the average lowest wages, the more full compensation is reduced. I also found that in the long-run, several industries experienced a significantly large increase in the quit rate: a result only possible if minimum wages reduce full compensation.

plete measure of the harmful effect of that "fringe benefit." Also, while increasing the minimum wage may not cause as much unemployment as sometimes claimed, the unemployment it does cause is even more perverse than commonly realized. There are some minimum-wage workers who are receiving little or no fringe benefits. These are the lowest paid of the lowest paid, and are the ones over whom the most concern is expressed when a minimum-wage increase is being debated. Yet they are the first ones employers will lay off when the minimum wage is increased. When the minimum wage is increased, there is no way employers can avoid an increase in the cost of hiring these workers since they have few, if any, fringe benefits to take away. So the unemployment that does occur from a hike in the minimum wage will be concentrated on the very workers advocates of the minimum wage claim are most in need of help.

Even without drawing parallels between minimum-wage legislation and mandated fringe benefits, the two interact in unfortunate ways. The unemployment effects of an increase in the minimum wage will be greater when fringe benefits are mandated, and therefore cannot be reduced. Also, the existence of a minimum wage reduces the ability of employers and entry-level workers to substitute fringe benefits for money in mutually advantageous ways. And when fringe benefits are mandated for minimum-wage workers with no non-mandated fringe benefits to reduce, higher labor costs are unavoidable, as is increased unemployment. Again, it is the lowest paid of the minimum-wage workers who end up unemployed. But it should not be forgotten that even those who keep their jobs are probably harmed by a minimum-wage increase.

SECURITY AGAINST "WRONGFUL" TERMINATION

Security against "wrongful" termination is another benefit that governments increasingly try to provide workers. This security is even less likely to be thought of as a mandated benefit than a minimum wage, since there is no single piece of legislation that requires employers to provide it. But there has been a host of court decisions and labor market legislation at every level of government aimed at making it more difficult for employers to dismiss workers. Under the employment-at-will doctrine that emerged out of the common law, and that still influences employment relations in the United States, an employer could terminate a worker without providing any justification (just as workers can terminate an employer by resigning without providing a justification). It is this doctrine that has been under judicial and legislative attack in recent decades in an attempt to provide workers more security. In a recent study of differences among state courts on the employment-at-will doctrine, Kesselring and Pittman (1993, p. 60) observe, "today, the employment-at-will doctrine has suffered significant erosion because of federal and state laws prohibiting employers from discriminating on the basis of race, color, religion, national origin, sex, age, and disability." According to Vedder and Gallaway (1995, p. 8), "During the 1980s, 32 states modified their view of the dismissal decision in the direction of accepting a more expansive interpretation of the constraints on the employment-at-will principle." So, given government's role in attempting to provide workers with job security against "wrongful" dismissal, it is reasonable to think of it as a mandated benefit.

Job security has other characteristics of more traditional mandated benefits. First, job security can be valuable to individual workers, but it is also a benefit that comes at a cost that workers cover through lower wages and/or other advantageous conditions of employment.

Second, employers have a strong motivation to provide more job security when it is worth more to workers than it costs to provide. And, as one would expect, employers in different industries, and different firms in the same industry, provide varying degrees of job security, allowing employers to sort themselves out in accordance with their aversion to risk. Construction jobs, for instance, provide less security than do jobs in education. As another example, Lincoln

Electric, an arc welder manufacturer in Cleveland, Ohio, despite being in an industry where layoffs are common, has a long history of never laying off a worker. But it requires its employees to work overtime during periods of heavy demand (thus avoiding having to hire more workers than it will need during the next down-cycle); guarantees only thirty hours of work per week during periods of slack demand; pays as much as 100 percent of a worker's compensation in a year-end bonus (which allows a lots of salary flexibility); and requires workers to shift job assignments (allowing management to shift workers from, say, production to sales during slack demand).[8]

Third, when government mandates job security, it imposes restrictions on labor market flexibility that harms the very workers supposedly being helped.

A strong argument can be made that the doctrine of employment-at-will does far more to promote the general interest of workers than does labor market regulation attempting to provide more job security. Employment-at-will does give the employer discretionary power. It gives the employee discretionary power as well, the power to quit. But the employee's power to quit is not at issue, so the question is how employers will use their employment-at-will power, given the incentives in the market place.

Competitive pressures motivate employers to use their power to hire and fire to secure the best workers they can at prevailing wages, and to discipline them by dismissing those whose productivity fails to meet expectations. Dismissed workers will often claim to be victims of an abusive labor practice, but, in fact, the employer's right to fire a worker is a right that will tend to be exercised on behalf of the general interest of workers, simply because doing so promotes the firm's profitability. While workers would prefer to avoid discipline themselves, they certainly want to work for a firm in which discipline is imposed on other workers. Only by being able to discipline its

---

8. For more on Lincoln Electric, see McKenzie and Lee (1998, pp. 91–92).

workers can a firm overcome the shirking and lack of team effort that would undermine its productivity and its ability to provide jobs at competitive wages. Hence, each worker is better off accepting discipline in return for making sure other workers are subjected to the same discipline.[9]

We are not denying that employer power under employment-at-will can be abused. All power is subject to abuse, including regulatory power concentrated in the hands of political authorities and their special-interest clients. And when politicians use their power to favor organized workers at the expense of workers in general, they do so with complete impunity. Indeed, they are rewarded. In contrast, employers who use their power to discharge employees unfairly risk establishing a reputation that makes it more costly to recruit good workers. Furthermore, this cost is greater for large firms hiring many workers (commonly considered to have the most power to exploit workers) than for small firms hiring few workers. Employees who are able and willing to provide value in their dealings with employers have far less to fear, and much more to gain, from the employment-at-will doctrine than from political control over labor markets.[10]

Neither are we denying that current employees can receive temporary advantage from political protections against normal market adjustments. This highly visible and immediate advantage makes it tempting to substitute the rigidity of regulation for the flexibility of

---

9. The point here is illustrated by the apocryphal story of the Chinese coolies who bought a barge to haul produce upstream, with each of them pulling the barge with a rope. To overcome the shirking problem, they hired a man to stand on the barge with a whip and lash anyone whose rope went slack. Even highly educated and motivated workers benefit from the discipline of a "boss," as evidenced by a true story. Gordon E. Moore, a chemist and one of the founders of Intel, tells of his experience, with seven other scientists, when they started Fairchild Semiconductor Corporation. Based on the chaos that the group had encountered in a previous venture, Moore (1994, p. 25) said that "the first thing we had to do was to hire our own boss—essentially hire someone to run the company."

10. For a powerful defense of employment-at-will, see Epstein (1984).

employment-at-will. The costs of this substitution are diffused and delayed and therefore easily ignored, or heavily discounted, politically. Much of these costs are spread over the entire population in the form of a less productive economy. But much of the costs are imposed on workers, supposedly the beneficiaries of the erosion of employment-at-will. How? By lowering employment opportunities and reducing the rewards from employment when it is received. Because these costs are widely dispersed, delayed, even unseen, and difficult to connect with the political policies that caused them, they are difficult to register politically.

For example, according to the study by Vedder and Gallaway (1995), the effect of wrongful termination laws caused a reduction in worker compensation of over $250 billion in 1993. Furthermore, low-income workers disproportionately suffered this loss. Vedder and Gallaway estimate that the move away from employment-at-will increased income inequality in the United States by over 10 percent (as measure by the Gini coefficient, a standard measure of income inequality). These losses and distortions are rarely connected with government restrictions on the freedom to contract. Indeed, they are far more likely to be blamed on some "market failure," or on employers who make the required adjustments in compensation. All too frequently, the resulting losses and distortions are used to justify yet more government restrictions on labor markets.

There should be no surprise in the finding that government restrictions on dismissing workers disproportionately harm low-income workers. Such restrictions have greatly increased the cost of hiring, as, generally, low-income workers are the least essential and therefore the easiest to avoid hiring. An important cost of substituting government regulations for employment-at-will is that of litigation. But it should be acknowledged that wrongful-dismissal litigation is actually quite rare, and the legal costs of such litigation amount to only about

0.1 percent of the total wage bill.[11] The real cost is not the direct cost of litigating wrongful dismissal suits, but the indirect costs of complying with the legal restriction imposed on labor-market decisions. There are the costs of diverting managers away from other activities to anticipate and protect against the consequences of litigation that are avoided. There are also the costs of retaining workers whose performance would justify dismissal if it were not for the threat of litigation, as well as the costs of the extra screening and background checks that could be avoided if correcting a poor hiring decision through dismissal was less costly.

Also, the restrictions on dismissal are only the foundation of what Epstein (1995, p. 161) calls a "regulatory pyramid" that stacks up compliance costs from regulations that would be avoided under employment-at-will. Regulators do not ignore the temptation facing employers to circumvent restrictions on firing by reducing an employee's pay, assigning unpleasant tasks or working hours, or requiring that the employee move to a less preferred location. The possibilities here are numerous and provide regulators with a justification for imposing on personnel decisions a host of regulations that ostensibly have nothing to do with dismissals. The costs of such regulatory meddling are far higher than the direct cost of litigation.

The magnitude of the total costs, both direct and indirect, of moving from employment-at-will to government regulation of hiring and firing decisions have been estimated by Dertouzos and Karoly (1992, chap. 6). These researchers estimate that employment has been reduced by 2 to 5 percent because of the wrongful termination liability threatened by regulation. Based on widely accepted wage elasticities of labor demand, this implies roughly a 10 percent increase in the cost of labor (Dertouzos and Karoly, 1992, chap. 6). If this cost of labor was saved (much of which could be saved by moving

11. See Dertouzos and Karoly (1992, p. xiii).

back to more reliance on employment-at-will), most of it would go into higher wages for workers and more products of better quality and lower prices for consumers. Workers and the general public are paying a high price for the mirage of worker protection provided by political intrusions into labor markets.

CONCLUSION

Almost every political intervention into labor markets concentrates benefits on an organized few by imposing a far greater cost on the unorganized many. Obviously, each benefiting group favors the intervention and is well positioned to exert political influence on its behalf by virtue of being relatively small and easily organized around a dominant interest. The political influence of each interest group is further enhanced by masquerading private advantage with a plausible sounding case that its proposal is good for all workers. Union members who favor health care coverage, for example, can reduce competition from younger workers who don't want or need such coverage by pushing legislation that mandates universal coverage, and do so with the rhetoric of public concern. This public-interest cover is crucial. No matter how much brute political muscle a special-interest group has, without some public-interest pretense its proposal will seldom achieve political liftoff. If the public did no more than apply the Kantian imperative (which requires that everyone be treated the same) and some elementary economic logic to political proposals, the morality and efficacy of most mandates would be quickly dismissed. This is certainly the case with government intrusions into labor markets. Those who benefit from the mandated protections provided by political restrictions on voluntary contracts between employers and employees would not want to live in an economy in which those protections were universally provided. Such an economy would quickly sink into poverty and stagnation because of the economy's inability to direct human effort and ingenuity into their most productive pursuits.

REFERENCES

Alpert, William T. "The Effects of the Minimum Wage on the Fringe Benefits of Restaurant Workers." Paper, Lehigh University, Bethlehem, PA, 1983.

Dertouzos, James N., and Lynn A. Karoly. *Labor Market Responses to Employer Liability.* Santa Monica, CA: Rand, 1992.

Dunn, L. F. "Nonpecuniary Job Preferences and Welfare Losses among Migrant Agriculture Workers." *American Journal of Agriculture Economics* 67 (May 1985): 257–65.

Epstein, Richard A. "In Defense of the Contract at Will." *University of Chicago Law Review* 51 (1984): 947–82.

———. *Simple Rules for a Complex World.* Cambridge, MA: Harvard University Press, 1995.

Fleisher, Belton M. *Minimum Wage Regulation in Retail Trade.* Washington, D.C.: American Enterprise Institute, 1981.

Hashimoto, Masanori. "Minimum Wage Effect on Training to the Job." *American Economic Review* 70 (December 1982): 1070–87.

Kesselring, Randall G., and Jeffrey R. Pittman. "Employment-at-Will: An Empirical Analysis." *Journal of Labor Research* 14 (Winter 1993): 59–67.

Lee, Dwight R. "Why Unions Support Mandated Benefits." *Journal of Labor Research* 18, no. 1 (Winter 1997): 111–19.

Lee, Dwight R., and Richard B. McKenzie. "Helping the Poor Through Government Poverty Programs: The Triumph of Rhetoric Over Reality." In *Public Choice and Constitutional Economics,* edited by James D. Gwartney and Richard E. Wagner, 387–408. Greenwich, CT.: JAI Press, Inc., 1988.

Leighton, Linda, and Jacob Mincer. "Effects of Minimum Wages on Human Capital Formation." In *The Economics of Legal Minimum Wages,* edited by Simon Rothenberg. Washington, D.C.: American Enterprise Institute, 1981.

Long, Stephen H., and M. Susan Marquis. *Gaps in Employment-Based*

Health Insurance: Lack of Supply and Lack of Demand, in Health Benefits and the Workforce. Washington, D.C.: U.S. Department of Labor, 1992.

McKenzie, Richard B., and Dwight R. Lee. *Managing Through Incentives: How to Develop a More Collaborative, Productive and Profitable Organization*. New York: Oxford University Press, 1998.

Moore, Gordon E. "The Accidental Entrepreneur." *Engineering & Science* 57 (Summer 1994): 23–30.

Smith, Adam. *The Theory of Moral Sentiments*. Indianapolis, IN: Liberty Fund, 1982.

Vedder, Richard, and Lowell Gallaway. "Laws, Litigation and Labor Markets: Some New Evidence." Report for the Pacific Research Institute for Public Policy, San Francisco, September 1995.

Wessels, Walter J. "Minimum Wages: Are Workers Better Off?" Paper presented at a conference on minimum wages, National Chamber Foundation, Washington, D.C., July 29, 1987.

CHAPTER FOUR

The Morality of
Labor Unions

Paul Heyne

A RECENT STATEMENT by the United States Conference of Catholic Bishops on Roman Catholic social teaching includes a short section on the Dignity of Work and the Rights of Workers. "If the dignity of work is to be protected," it asserts, "then the basic rights of workers must be respected—the right to productive work, to decent and fair wages, to organize and join unions, to private property, and to economic initiative."[1] This chapter will wander between economics and ethics to explore a question that the bishops would probably consider outrageous: Why should the right to organize and join unions be one of the basic rights of workers that people interested in social justice are bound to respect?

---

1. "Sharing Catholic Social Teaching: Challenges and Directions," reflections of the U.S. Catholic Bishops, August 26, 1998.

ECONOMICS AND ETHICS

Economics and ethics is a combination that many economists deem no more possible than oil and water. In what is probably the most influential essay on the methodology of economics ever published, Lionel Robbins insisted that there was no defensible way to mix economics and ethics. "Economics," he wrote, "deals with ascertainable facts; ethics with valuations and obligations. The two fields of inquiry are not on the same plane of discourse." Ethics talks about what ought to be, and economics about what is. "Propositions involving the word 'ought' are different in kind," Robbins insisted, "from propositions involving the word 'is.' And it is difficult to see what possible good can be served by not keeping them separate, or failing to recognize their essential difference."[2]

Robbins was writing during the 1930s at the high tide of logical positivism, with its confident presumption that clear distinctions vigorously enforced could sweep away many of the confusions infecting both science and politics as a result of centuries of wishful thinking. By keeping economics completely separate from ethics, the discussion of means distinct from the discussion of ends, we could supposedly do a better job of resolving our differences. "In the rough-and-tumble of political struggle," Robbins wrote,

> differences of opinion may arise either as a result of differences about ends or as a result of differences about the means of attaining ends. Now, as regards the first type of difference, neither Economics nor any other science can provide any solvent. If we disagree about ends it is a case of thy blood or mine—or live and let live, according to the importance of the difference, or the relative strength of our opponents.

2. Lionel Robbins, *An Essay on the Nature and Significance of Economic Science*, 2d ed., revised and extended (London: Macmillan and Company, Ltd., 1952), pp. 148–49. Robbins's *Essay* was originally published in 1932 and republished in revised form in 1935.

But if we disagree about means, then scientific analysis can often help us to resolve our differences.[3]

But the relationship between ends and means is not as clear and simple as all that. We each choose some ends while rejecting others in part on the basis of whether we believe ourselves in command of the means for reaching them, and we disagree among ourselves about the value of particular ends in large part because we disagree about whether we have the means to attain them. Robbins says that when we disagree about ultimate ends, it is a matter of "thy blood or mine" if the issue is important to us. But the truth is that we much more often discuss disagreements about ends than we resort to violence. And when we engage in discussion, we rely heavily on facts and reason to make our case, just as scientists do. We point out that this end deserves a greater weight than that one because this one supports some other end of importance to all of us, or that the superior worth of a particular end that we share is largely canceled out by the improbability of our being able to attain it. "It doesn't work that way" is a very common argument in ethical discussions, an argument that is surely as much (or more) in the realm of means as in the realm of ends.

It might be the case that we would have to resort to force to settle the issue if we disagreed about *ultimate* ends. But how often does that occur? It is hard to think of any end, goal, objective, or value that is truly ultimate, that cannot be argued for. The abortion issue probably divides Americans more deeply at the present time than any other issue in the public forum. The division would not be as deep and unresolvable if we did not choose to frame the question in terms of stark alternatives, such as the right to life versus the right to choose. Surely both ends are valuable and worthy of protection. Those who debate the abortion issue are actually divided on the

3. Ibid., p. 150.

relative weights to be assigned to ends and values that both sides generally share, weights that almost everyone will want to adjust with varying circumstances. We elevate particular values because we believe they serve other values. But whether or not they actually do so is often a question open to analysis and discussion, processes that can be facilitated with information drawn from one or another of the sciences.

Economics and ethics do not in fact inhabit completely separate realms of discourse, and keeping them rigorously apart will not help us to resolve our political differences.

THE ECONOMICS OF COLLECTIVE BARGAINING

Labor unions have served many purposes, but their primary goal, and the one with which we begin, is raising the net compensation of their members. Unions campaign for members by promising to make them "better off" in ways that will presumably impose additional costs on employers. Assuming that employers aren't simply spiteful, they are always willing to make their employees better off if doing so has no cost. But employers aim at increasing net revenue, which is receipts minus wages and other costs, and this sets them at least partially in opposition to their employees, for whom wages are not costs but income. "In union there is strength" has been the constant motto of labor unions, because strength is needed to resist the efforts of employers to enhance profits at the expense of wages.

This model, which depicts employers and employees as engaged in a struggle over division of the product, is implicitly supported in the prelude to the Wagner Act, the original National Labor Relations Act passed by Congress in 1935 to strengthen labor unions:

> The inequality of bargaining power between employees who do not possess full freedom of association or actual liberty of contract, and employers who are organized in the corporate or other forms of ownership association substantially burdens and affects the flow of com-

merce, and tends to aggravate recurrent business depressions, by depressing wage rates and the purchasing power of wage earners in industry and by preventing the stabilization of competitive wage rates and working conditions within and between industries.

While the "findings and policy" sections of bills must always be taken with a grain of salt, this one does manage to state a presupposition widely held among the general public, that wage rates are determined by the relative bargaining power of employees and employers.

Economic theory offers a more complex perspective. Employers have a demand for labor that reflects the estimated marginal contribution that workers will make to the net revenue of their firms. It is the marginal contribution that determines the demand: the amount of net revenue that a potential worker will add to the firm's net revenue, given everything else, including the number of workers already being employed. The more workers there are already employed, other things being equal, the smaller will be the expected contribution to net revenue of an additional worker. This implies that the lower the cost of obtaining workers, the higher the number employers will want to hire. It also implies that the more workers will be able to secure a higher wage, other things again remaining equal, the fewer will be the number of qualified workers available for hire. Wage rates are determined, in other words, by the interaction of demand and supply.

The implications of the economist's perspective become clearer when we ask what this perspective denies or rules out. To begin with, it denies that employers will want to hire a specific number of employees, the number they "need" to run the operation, regardless of what they must pay to obtain them. It suggests, on the contrary, that the size and nature of the operation will itself depend in part on the cost of obtaining workers. Thus, fast-food outlets, for example, do not *require* any specific number of employees. If a very high wage must be paid to obtain competent personnel, fast-food outlets will be open only at the busiest hours, customers will wait longer for service, and there will be fewer such outlets in operation.

The bargaining-power theory of wage determination tends to assume that the demand for workers is completely inelastic with respect to the cost of hiring. Each employer needs some definite number of employees, a number basically fixed by technology, and will hire that number at a very low wage rate or at a very high wage rate, at least until the wage rate becomes so high that the employer is compelled to shut down the business. Between this shut-down rate and some minimum rate below which workers will prefer to remain unemployed, the relative bargaining power of employers and employees sets the actual wage rate that will be paid. Within this model, labor unions, by increasing the bargaining power of employees, redistribute income from employers to employees.

The economist's model carries different implications. The most important is that the wage rate will be set by the number of workers willing and able to supply their services. If fast-food outlets offer a high wage to unskilled workers, so many will offer to work that the quantity supplied will exceed the quantity demanded and employers will have to ration the available positions. To ration means to allocate according to some kind of discriminatory criteria. The law rules out some kinds of discrimination, but the legal criteria include such usually advantageous (for the employer) discriminatory criteria as education, previous experience, recommendations, personal appearance, and prior acquaintance. The most important potential criterion for discriminating among job applications may be the willingness to work for less. If the employer is interested in increasing net revenue, the last criterion will seem especially advantageous and the high wage rate will fall in response to competition.

This, of course, is the competition that unions try to control or prevent. Employees do not compete against employers but against one another, and it is a primary objective of labor unions to restrict competition between workers with the goal of raising wage rates or keeping them high. A union that can compel employers to hire only union members can restrict competition by making it difficult for potential employees to join the union, either directly or by establishing onerous and time-consuming procedures for acquiring the qualifications for membership. Since 1947 unions have been legally barred from enforcing contracts that require prior union membership as a condition of hiring, a prohibition that makes the unions' task more difficult.

A union that succeeds in negotiating a high wage for its members, a wage at which the quantity of qualified labor supplied significantly exceeds the quantity that employers demand, will thereby create a pool of qualified potential competitors for the jobs of its members. This competition will weaken the union's bargaining position when the time comes to negotiate a new contract because the alternative of "going nonunion" will appear more feasible to the employer.

It follows that the unions able to negotiate the highest wage rates for members will be the unions representing workers with valuable skills that are difficult to acquire. These, however, will be workers who would tend to be well compensated even in the absence of a union. Health care organizations offer high wages to the physicians whom they hire because they could not otherwise obtain the employees they want. Electricians would earn much more than file clerks whether or not electricians were unionized. And file clerks will probably not be able to raise their earnings appreciably by forming a union because any significant improvement in their position will attract a flood of new applicants who will weaken the union's bargaining position.

This is why economists have historically been skeptical about both the claims of supporters that unions have greatly improved the position of workers and the claims of opponents that unions have done grave damage to the economy. The economist's model of wage determination suggests that in the long run unions will not be able greatly to affect relative wage rates or the distribution of income between owners of businesses and their employees.

TESTING THE MODEL

"In the long run" is a useful phrase for anyone who wants to generalize without fear of empirical refutation. In economics, the long run sometimes seems to mean a period of time long enough to make the generalization irrefutable. Has the impact of unions on the distribution of income really been as limited as our argument suggests? Were the efforts of the various craft unions associated after the 1880s in the American Federation of Labor (AFL), of the United Mineworkers of America under the legendary John L. Lewis, of the United Automobile Workers and the United Steel Workers beginning in the 1930s, or of the American Federation of State, County, and Municipal Employees in recent years been simply much ado about very little?

A brief look at each of the cases mentioned may help to clarify the analysis and indicate some of its limitations. The history of craft unions in the United States, such as the various unions representing workers in the construction trades, seems to confirm the analysis. These unions were able to negotiate high wages for their members early on because their members possessed valuable skills that were relatively difficult to acquire. The unions also developed and deployed a variety of tactics to prevent nonunion workers who did acquire the requisite skills from offering their services in competition with union members. Racial exclusions, enforced by contract, custom, threat, or even legislation, were an important tactic in the North as well as the South. So was mutual support among the craft unions; by prohibiting their members from crossing picket lines erected by other unions, the various craft unions made it more difficult for employers to hire nonunion labor even when it was abundantly available. And until they were made illegal in 1947 by the Labor-Management Relations Act (Taft-Hartley Act), closed shop contracts prevented employers from gradually substituting less expensive employees for union members. The steadily declining percentage of unionized workers over the past two or three decades in trades traditionally dominated by the craft unions of the old AFL would be a predictable consequence of laws banning the closed shop, restricting such mutual support tactics as secondary strikes and boycotts, and suppressing racial and gender discrimination.

The United Mineworkers Union under the formidable John L. Lewis secured dramatic improvements in the wages and working conditions of coal miners between the 1920s and the 1940s, improvements that almost surely would not have occurred in the absence of the union. In this case the exception proves the rule. Lewis openly avowed his intention to eliminate coal mining jobs by raising the cost of hiring coal miners and, thereby, forcing the mine owners to substitute machinery for labor, thus accomplishing simultaneously the twin objectives of reducing the number of people employed in an unhealthful and dangerous occupation while improving the lives of those who remained in that occupation.

Automobile workers and steel workers were the aristocrats of semi-skilled labor for a number of years after World War II, thanks to the efforts of the United Automobile Workers (UAW) and the United Steel Workers (USW). The founders and leaders of these noncraft unions took full advantage of the favorable environment created for them by the 1935 Wagner Act. This act imposed upon employers a legal duty to bargain collectively and outlawed as unfair labor practices many of the most effective devices that employers had regularly used to resist unionization of their enterprises. Once certified by the National Labor Relations Board as the exclusive bargaining agent for everyone employed by each automobile or steel manufacturer, the UAW and the USW used the strike threat to secure wage rates that were the envy of manufacturing workers elsewhere. They negotiated union shop contracts, under which workers must join the union when they are hired, as a way to make sure that the high wages accrued to their members. By organizing all the firms in the industry, these unions prevented the erosion of their gains through competition from nonunionized domestic firms. Competition from foreign manufacturers was, for a time, effectively controlled by successful lobbying for tariffs and other restrictions on imports. The power of the UAW and the USW diminished, however, and the differential advantages of the workers they represented shrank correspondingly when foreign automobile manufacturers and small, nonunionized steel mills took advantage of high labor costs to undersell the large corporations organized by the UAW and the USW. The once munificent wages of automobile and steel workers have proved to be a major cause of high unemployment rates in areas such as Detroit and Pittsburgh, where very high wages came to be regarded as the norm.

Almost all United States unions, craft and industrial, have suffered severe membership losses over the past twenty years. A marked exception is the American Federation of State, County, and Municipal Employees. The AFSCME has attracted loyal members by bargaining successfully for improved compensation and benefits in a period when other unions were being forced to moderate their demands and were losing members, often through having priced themselves out of the market. The percentage of unionized firms in the building trades, for example, has declined in a striking fashion. This is true even for some regions with strong union traditions, as unionized contractors increasingly found themselves unable to match the job bids of contractors who had shifted to nonunion labor. The AFSCME bargains, however, with employers who generally don't face much competition: state, county, and municipal governments. It is harder to obtain a wage increase from an employer who must recover any higher costs by increasing prices to customers who have good alternatives than it is to obtain a wage increase from an employer who can extract additional revenue from clients who have no option except to pay their taxes. Economic theory predicts that the AFSCME will do less well in the future as "tax revolts" increasingly threaten elected officials, and that it will continue to lobby hard against "contracting out" of government services. The competition that causes employers to hire fewer workers when wage costs rise can and does take many forms. Even governments are not exempt.

QUESTIONS OF JUSTICE: A FIRST LOOK

In striving to increase the job compensation of their members, labor unions are certainly intending to alter the distribution of the goods and services produced by the economic system. Just *how* they alter it, however, is a much more complex question than either the friends or the foes of labor unions traditionally assume.

When the United Widget Workers Union increases the labor costs of the Wedgwood Widget Company, Wedgwood acquires an incentive to produce widgets at a somewhat lesser rate and to increase its price by some amount. By how much will depend on the price elasticity of the demand for its widgets, or how responsive its customers are to price increases. If all the widget makers with whom Wedgwood competes are subjected to the same increase in labor costs, and if there are no decent substitutes for widgets, Wedgwood could end up raising the price of its widgets by an amount close to its additional wage cost per widget. If Wedgwood's competitors are nonunion and their labor costs do not increase, or if good substitutes for Wedgwood's widgets are readily available (the best substitute for a Wedgwood widget will be another maker's widget), Wedgwood may have an incentive to reduce output substantially or even to give up widget production altogether. In that case, the increased compensation that the UWWU obtains will benefit only those of its members who continue to work for Wedgwood, and they will obtain their gains partially, perhaps largely, at the expense of those who no longer have jobs with Wedgwood.

Widget consumers will also lose, obtaining fewer widgets and paying a higher price for them. The owners of Wedgwood will take some of the loss because Wedgwood's net revenue will decline. Wedgwood's suppliers will also be somewhat worse off. The town in which Wedgwood is located might find its tax base diminished. Anyone with the slightest understanding of how a market system functions and who takes the time to think the matter through will realize that the UWWU does not simply make its members better off at the expense of Wedgwood's shareholders, who might include, just to highlight the uncertainty and ambiguity of the effects, the workers' own pension fund.

Advocates of increased minimum legal wages often say that they would be perfectly willing to pay more for a burger or a cotton shirt in order to provide a living wage to the workers who produce burgers and cotton shirts. But would they go on purchasing *as many* burgers or cotton shirts as they formerly purchased? Even if they would, would everyone else do the same? A market system is a social system in which it is rarely possible to alter one variable without affecting others. Actions have unintended and unanticipated consequences.

Members of the building trades unions in the United States long enjoyed rates of compensation that were the envy of workers elsewhere. They did not do so, however, at the expense of wealthy capitalists. Their benefits were obtained at the cost of higher housing prices and, hence, less new housing, as well as at the expense of workers excluded either directly or indirectly from participation in the construction industry. When the lobbying efforts of construction unions secured federal legislation that required all contractors working on federally funded projects to pay "prevailing wages," with "prevailing wages" defined as union scale, unionized contractors were protected against competition on government jobs from nonunion contractors. That was, of course, the goal of the unions' lobbying efforts. But the goal was attained partly at the expense of taxpayers and partly at the expense of workers excluded from opportunities for employment on government jobs.

Labor unions succeed in raising the compensation of their members insofar as they can protect the jobs of their members against competition from nonunion workers. If this is correct, why should people interested in social justice be bound to respect the right of workers to organize and join unions? Would people interested in social justice be equally bound to respect the right of grocery store owners to organize and join trade associations, especially if the associations' goal was to raise prices and protect their members against competition from new stores that wanted to enter the industry? What makes the cases so different that our laws actively support the organization of unions while outlawing the organization of trade associations that try to fix prices or restrict entry?

ASSURING COMPETENCE

If unions did nothing except try to increase the labor costs of employers, we would not find many employers actively supporting unions. We do find such employers because unions perform other functions as well.

The building trades unions have long operated apprenticeship systems that provide employers in their industry with a continuing supply of skilled and certified workers. The unions' claims that those who hire their members are assured of competent employees and that hiring nonunion workers can be risky are not mere propaganda. Of course, an organization that wants employers to hire exclusively from the ranks of its members will have an interest in providing a continuing supply and in monitoring the competence of those whom it provides. Moreover, by operating the training system for its industry, the unions in the building trades made it easier for themselves to reserve these well-compensated jobs for those whom they favored, such as white males exclusively and preferably the sons and nephews of current union members.

There is another question to be raised. Is a more competent worker always to be preferred to a less competent one? We would all want strong assurances of high competence levels on the part of the electricians who are installing new circuit breakers in our home. Would we also be willing to pay union wages to have an electrician attach new plates on our light switches? When greater competence means higher costs, greater competence will not always be preferable. We should not send a boy to do a man's job, as the old saying has it; neither should we send a man to do a boy's job. A system that guarantees competence can easily become a system that forces people to pay for more than they really want or require. A pretended dedication to public safety or consumer protection, by business firms even more than by craft unions, has often functioned as the justification for government-enforced restrictions on competition.

GRIEVANCE SYSTEMS

The widespread belief that labor unions are responsible for the high wages generally prevailing in wealthy nations largely reflects a failure to understand the market forces that prompt employers to pay workers close to what they are worth, or, to be more precise, to pay them the value of their net contribution to the revenue of the enterprise. If a firm can obtain workers for $10 an hour who each hour add $15 worth of value to the company's product, the firm will ordinarily want to hire more such workers. These differences between workers' value to employers and their cost to employers—closely akin to what Karl Marx dubbed "surplus value"—creates an incentive to hire more workers. Increasing productivity thus generates an increased demand for workers that continually pulls wages up toward the value of the workers' output.

The market system does a less effective job of protecting workers against other forms of exploitation, such as arbitrary and unfair treatment by a supervisor. Even in a highly competitive labor market, workers who are disciplined or demoted or discharged because a foreman took a dislike to them will often have to incur substantial costs to find fair treatment with another employer. That is why a good grievance system, operated by the union that represents all the employees in the collective bargaining unit, can be so important. The "inequality of bargaining power" of which the Wagner Act speaks can be a serious problem when employees work under supervisors who are petty tyrants.

Employers, of course, do not want their employees to feel resentful because they believe themselves to have been unfairly treated. Employers naturally prefer high employee morale, a cooperative spirit, and feelings of loyalty toward the employer. A good grievance system can nurture all of these, or at least retard the growth of their opposites. Many employers have expressed a willingness to trade off the reduction in the degree of their control over job conditions that unionization entails in order to obtain the employee grievance system that unionization also brings with it.

DEMOCRACY AND LABOR UNIONS

But what if the union representatives fail to do an effective job of prosecuting an employee's grievance? An employee might be irritating to a shop steward as well as to a foreman. Or union representatives might be willing to sell out their membership for the sake of some personal advantage. Complaints of unfair treatment directed by union members against their own unions are not unknown. The Labor-Management Reporting and Disclosure Act of 1959, known as the Landrum-Griffin Act, gained considerable support from the belief that unions often exercised a tyranny of their own over those whom they were supposed to protect.

There have certainly been corrupt union officials and even entire unions, or at least union locals, that were riddled with corruption. A union such as the Teamsters, which represents transportation workers (among many others), has the ability to inflict large damages on selected employers at a relatively small cost to itself or its membership. It can do so by interfering with the movement of supplies or finished products at critical times and in ways that appear, on the surface, to be completely legitimate. That ability creates the power to practice extortion, and the power to practice extortion attracts criminals. The Teamsters union, with its long history of corruption, does not so much breed corrupt union officials as attract criminals who find union power an effective means toward personal enrichment.

It would be a mistake to suppose that more democracy, mandated by legislation and monitored by special government overseers, will be an effective cure for this problem. The strategic position that enables corrupt union officials to enrich themselves through extortion also enables honest union officials to secure benefits for their members. Members of the Teamsters union consequently have been far less dissatisfied with their leadership than members of Congress, crusading journalists, or concerned citizens, and have sometimes voted right back into office officials who were earlier removed by the government for "undemocratic" behavior.

Campaigns for more democratic procedures in labor unions are often supported, it should be noted, by people with a record of opposition to labor unions, and for good reason. Democratic collective bargaining is likely to be as ineffective as democratic foreign policy making, because democratic procedures make strategic ploys more difficult, if not impossible. They tip the hand of the union bargaining team and reveal some of the weaknesses in the union's position, making it harder to bluff and narrowing the space for compromise and accommodation in directions disadvantageous to the union.

When public policy forces union leaders to pay more attention to minority opinion in the union, it also reduces the union's ability to overcome the free rider problem. It will always be in the self-interest of a union member, at least if we conceive self-interest very narrowly, to let others pay the dues and bear the costs of a strike. Loyalty to the union and firm support for its policies are essential parts of a union's strength. That strength begins to dissolve when dissidents obtain the right to refrain from supporting union policies without penalty or to employ union resources to argue for positions opposed by the union leadership. No one wants to take a stand against democracy. But democracy can take many forms, and some are simply not compatible with union strength.

LABOR UNIONS AND INEQUALITY

But why should we be interested in union strength? What is it about labor unions that should make those interested in justice eager to enhance the bargaining power of unions?

The reviewer of a recent biography of the late Supreme Court Justice Thurgood Marshall praises Marshall in these words:

> No member of the Supreme Court has ever been more keenly alive to social inequalities. For twenty-four years, in a few notable opinions for the Court, and many impassioned dissents, Marshall consistently supported organized labor, racial minorities, the advancement of women, the broadening of rights to freedom of expression, and the narrowing of police authority.[4]

Does organized labor belong in that list? Do labor unions reduce social inequalities?

From the 1880s, when the American Federation of Labor was created, to the 1930s, when the rival Congress of Industrial Organizations was created, labor unions in America generally represented the more skilled and better paid workers in the country. Union advocates claimed, of course, that their members were better paid because they were represented by unions. We are closer to the truth

4. Randall Kennedy, review of Juan Williams's biography of Thurgood Marshall, *The New Republic*, April 5, 1999, p. 39.

when we say they were represented by unions because they were better paid. It would be most correct to say that they were better paid *and* represented by unions because they possessed relatively high skill levels that made it hard for employers to replace them when they went on strike.

It is difficult for a union representing unskilled workers to bargain successfully for higher wages, because such a union cannot make a credible strike threat. Employers can too easily replace workers who go on strike. Even if the union is able to prevent the replacement of strikers and to compel the employer to pay a higher wage, the gain is likely to be a short-term one. With workers available for a wage below the union wage, nonunion firms will be able to chip away at the net revenue of the unionized firm, prohibiting it from charging a higher price to help cover its higher labor costs.

Wage rates in the United States have shown a pattern of increasing inequality over the past two decades, a phenomenon that some commentators have attributed to the decline of union strength. Once again, though, it would seem that an association may have been identified incorrectly with a cause. The industries in which union members tended to be most heavily concentrated have declined as a percentage of the total economy as production has moved increasingly in the direction of services. Some of this decline has undoubtedly been a consequence of the relatively high costs that unions have imposed. From 1980 to 1995, membership in the automobile workers union declined by 45 percent and membership in the steelworkers union by 67 percent, not because union members were a smaller percentage of the workforce in unionized plants, but because unionized plants were hiring fewer workers.[5]

The once powerful building trades unions also suffered major

5. Data on union membership were taken from *Statistical Abstract of the United States*, which reproduces them from the biennial *Report of the AFL-CIO Executive Council*.

membership losses over this period. Membership in the carpenters union fell by 52 percent, membership in the electrical craft union by 35 percent, and membership in the plumbers union by 37 percent. The basic reason was the growth of nonunion contractors.

But isn't this evidence of declining union strength? Not necessarily. We want to distinguish between membership losses due to a decline in union strength and membership losses due to the exercise of union strength, that is, to unions pricing their members' services out of the market.

If union strength declined between 1980 and 1995 because public attitudes and government policy turned against unions during this period, we should expect to see membership declines in unions of government employees. We find on the contrary that membership in the two teachers unions, the National Education Association and the American Federation of Teachers, increased by 28 percent, and membership in the American Federation of State, County, and Municipal Employees rose 8 percent. Combined membership in the letter carriers and postal workers unions fell by 2 percent from 1980 to 1995, but that is inconsequential when compared to the size of the losses in most of the unions that bargain with private employers.

When nonunion contractors take over jobs that were formerly performed by union contractors, does inequality increase? Does the average wage paid by contractors decline? No clear answer can be given. A loss of jobs by members of the International Brotherhood of Electrical Workers to nonunion electricians will *reduce* inequality among electricians. Inequality among airline pilots clearly declines when new airlines, paying pilots half the wage rate that the pilots union has negotiated with the major carriers, expand by taking business away from the major carriers.

Mention of the airline pilots union raises the question in vivid form. If we choose to think of organized airline pilots as regular union members, we would not want to assume automatically that every increase in the wage rate paid to union members diminishes income inequality. The gains achieved for their members by powerful unions that organize highly-skilled workers distribute income from poor to rich insofar as they restrict entry of workers into their trades.

There are unions that have shown a particular concern for employees receiving very low wages and working under especially unpleasant conditions. The United Farmworkers of the late Cesar Chavez come to mind. But such unions are very far from representative of unions generally. There seems to be no good reason to assume that unions play a significant role in reducing income inequality in the United States.

INEQUALITY AND INJUSTICE

"Inequality" is not a synonym for "inequity." Whether a particular inequality is also an inequity will depend on our conception of justice. Whereas achieving agreement among people on what constitutes "justice" is a notoriously difficult task, it is much easier to discover a consensus on the meaning of "injustice."

There is no defensible way to attach a specific numerical value to the concept of "a fair wage." However the concept is defined, its monetary value will vary hugely with time and place. The "social activists" who want American apparel firms to pay a fair wage to their employees in manufacturing establishments in underdeveloped countries do not expect them to pay a wage even remotely close to what the average American worker receives. Those activists who believe that the differences they are willing to tolerate reflect differences in living costs are deluding themselves. Wage rates are lower in Indonesia than in the United States because workers in Indonesia are willing to accept less; they are willing to accept less because their alternative opportunities are so much poorer; their alternative opportunities are poorer than the alternative opportunities available to American workers because the marginal productivity of workers in the United States is far higher than the corresponding productivity of Indonesian workers; and the differences in productivity at the relevant margins reflect the much greater productivity of the economic system in the United States.

An American shoe or apparel firm with a factory abroad might easily be capable of paying its foreign employees a wage rate equal to what it pays in the United States. But if it had to do so, it would have no incentive to open a factory there—which would leave its foreign employees worse off. Moreover, an American firm offering ordinary semiskilled operatives seven dollars an hour in Indonesia would find itself flooded with job applicants. How would it choose the tiny percentage of them whom it would want to hire? And how would it justify this transfer of wealth from the shareholders of the firm to a small and arbitrarily selected set of Indonesian workers? Those who are the sole owners of the firms they manage have a right to distribute the wealth of their enterprise pretty much as they choose. But arbitrary decisions on the part of those who manage companies owned by others will not be tolerated long if those decisions reduce the value of the companies. The managers will be violating fiduciary obligations in order to satisfy charitable inclinations that are not truly charitable, because their inclinations are leading them to give away other people's money.

Can we even talk sensibly about a fair wage just within the specific context of the United States at the beginning of the twenty-first century? How would we define it? A wage sufficient to support a family? Such a wage would exclude from employment those whose skills and experience do not make them worth that much to an employer, such as teenagers who don't have families to support. The same wage for everyone? That would not work for reasons too obvious to list. A wage that meets the employee's needs? Consider the implications of a wage policy that allocates three times as much to an employee with seven children and an invalid spouse as to an unmarried employee with spartan tastes. The customary wage? A wage that the employee considers fair? A wage of which the employer is not ashamed? We are getting closer.

Suppose we turn the question around and ask what might be meant by "an unfair wage"? We can begin to make a little progress when we approach the question from this direction. A wage would clearly be unfairly low if it was less than had been agreed upon, or if fraud or deception had played a part in its determination, or if the wage was agreed upon under coercion. In introducing the concept of coercion we raise the troublesome question of whether someone can be coerced by circumstances. Is a worker who has no good alternative opportunities being coerced? Suppose my university is able to hire foreign undergraduate students to perform highly skilled work for no more than the legal minimum wage because American immigration law will only permit them to accept work related to their education and they are in urgent need of income. Is the university coercing them? Is it taking advantage of the fact that they must either work for the university or not work at all? Or is the university making them better off by providing them with an opportunity to work when otherwise they would have no opportunity at all? Or is it both coercing them and making them better off?

We can always find complicating circumstances to raise doubts about simple definitions. I shall nonetheless suggest a simple definition of a fair wage. It is a wage agreed upon by employer and employee under circumstances that are not unfair. And what are unfair circumstances? They are circumstances that violate the generally understood and accepted rules: the laws, conventions, and reigning moral consensus of the society in which we live. If that seems much too vague to be useful, I suggest that any definition that tries to become less vague will prove increasingly ambiguous as efforts are made to render it more specific.

TWO KINDS OF JUSTICE?

Reinhold Niebuhr introduced an important distinction into ethical discourse in the 1930s that has subsequently been largely forgotten in the moral and religious communities to which he, as a theologian, was primarily addressing himself. In his 1932 book on *Moral Man and Immoral Society*, Niebuhr argued that collectives are less moral than individuals and that reason, religion, and moral suasion are consequently less effective against collectives than they are against individuals. Niebuhr concluded that collectives must consequently be restrained by power if injustice is to be checked, and that conscience and reason, though they may modify struggles between collectives, can never be completely adequate substitutes for power.[6]

Niebuhr was basically arguing for two different concepts of justice. Justice in families or in small intentional communities will require that everyone receive what contributes to their full flourishing insofar as the resources of the group will allow it. If available resources are inadequate, they must be shared in a manner that takes into account the specific past and future prospects, needs and abilities, of each member of the group and of the group as a whole. The pursuit of justice in this sense presupposes a degree of knowledge and specific concern that cannot exist except in relatively small groups. A more limited concept of justice must be employed in social relationships outside of small societies in which everyone is capable of knowing and caring for specific others.

Niebuhr did not push his analysis far enough. He was impressed by the lack of any conscience in collectives and the consequent need to erect some kind of checks upon the exercise of group power that

6. Reinhold Niebuhr, *Moral Man and Immoral Society: A Study in Ethics and Politics* (New York: Charles Scribner's Sons, 1949). Original publication was in 1932.

would be more effective than mere moral exhortation. He does not seem to have noticed a deeper dimension to the problem, namely, the absence of personal relationships in the collective encounters with which he was largely concerned. Most of the relationships among people who interact in modern, urban societies are almost wholly impersonal. We typically know very little about the people, for example, on whom we depend every day for the food we eat, i.e., those who grow it, transport it, process it, and sell it to us. At most we may know the face and perhaps the first name of the person at the checkout counter in the grocery store. We consequently could not assume responsibility for the well-being of those whose services provide for our own well-being, even if we wanted to. We would not know enough about them. How could we even begin to compare the relative needs of all those people who feed us so that we might be able to share our wealth equitably with them? The very idea is absurd. We cannot be responsible for them.

This unavoidable "irresponsibility" is fully reciprocal. Those who grow, transport, and process our food know nothing about us and, as a result, cannot decide to provide our daily bread because they care about our nutrition. They take their cues not from our needs or wants but from the wholly impersonal signals that monetary prices provide. To put it crudely, they do what they do because they expect it to pay them better than anything else they might do.

What does justice mean in this world of completely impersonal transactions? If we take the most general definition of justice—giving to each their due—how do we decide what each is due? In such a world the Golden Rule is simply irrelevant. Social transactions in a market-coordinated economy cannot be governed by the principle "Do for others what you would like them to do for you." The appropriate rule is what someone has called the Silver Rule: "Do not do to others anything that you would consider unfair if they did it to you."

And what is unfair? Most people will shrug their shoulders hopelessly if asked, "What is fair?" But we know surprisingly well what is *un*fair. It is violating the rules by which we have agreed to be bound in our social relationships.

The concept of distributive justice has almost no relevance in a market economy. The only justice we can hope to secure is procedural justice, which we pursue by correcting perceived injustices. Injustices are committed when people violate the rules, when they fail to accord others due process.

An obvious question immediately arises: Can't the rules themselves be unjust? Indeed they can. But how do we recognize an unjust rule? It would be a rule that violates a deeper rule, which might itself be unjust if it violates a still deeper and more fundamental rule.

Anyone who objects that this entails an infinite regress should note that this is, in fact, how almost everyone thinks about justice whenever they are concerned with actual cases and not merely engaged in academic discussion. We may think and talk like complete relativists when we are asked what justice requires, but we display passion and confident conviction when we discern injustice. Injustice will almost invariably turn out to entail a violation of some right that an individual or group possesses. Where do these rights come from? They are created by the acceptance of obligations, by the explicit and implicit promises that we make to one another, by the "social contract" under which we live.

THE JUSTICE OF CONCERTED ACTION

A fair wage, then, to return to the point where this discussion began, is any wage upon which employer and employee agree so long as no injustice has been done.

Would that include wages determined by collective bargaining? In the nineteenth century, the common law doctrine of conspiracy led the courts to look askance at any concerted action intended to harm another. Those doctrines found statutory expression in the 1890 Sherman Act, which prohibited contracts, combinations, and conspiracies in restraint of trade, and in similar legislative enactments by state governments. After half a century of vacillating on the issue of whether combinations of employees fell under the prohibitions of federal "antitrust law," the Supreme Court finally decided that they did not. The Court said that Congress had clearly shown through the labor legislation passed in the 1930s its intention to exempt labor unions from the Sherman Act's prohibition of contracts, combinations, and conspiracies in restraint of trade. And under the preemption rule whereby federal legislation in an area trumps all state legislation in that same area, the Court's decision authorized labor unions to engage in practices that were *prima facie* illegal when engaged in by business firms.

Some critics of labor unions have proclaimed this an indefensible double standard. Most people haven't thought about it, and those few who have done so generally conclude that the inequality of bargaining power to which the Wagner Act referred justifies the double standard. The economic analysis of collective bargaining presented earlier in this chapter suggests that the best response might be to ignore the issue. Concerted action among employees organized into labor unions can restrict to some extent the competition among employees that works to keep wages down, but it cannot restrict competition effectively enough to prevent labor markets from allocating resources with reasonable efficiency and fairness. In recent years, critics of the Sherman Act have begun calling for its repeal on the grounds that ordinary market competition is sufficient to prevent concerted action by business firms from doing the damage to the economy that advocates of the act have always feared. If this conclusion came to be generally accepted, the alleged double standard would be eliminated by exempting business firms as well as employees from statutory prohibitions of concerted action.

The ordinary laws would still apply, however. That must be added because competition becomes markedly less effective in preventing the acquisition of excessive power when the competitors can employ violence or the threat of it. If business firms can assassinate those who try to compete with them or torch their establishments and hijack their shipments, they will find it much easier to charge very high prices and still obtain large net revenues. Similarly, if workers can employ violence or the threat of violence against those who try to compete with them, they will find it easier to obtain and sustain for longer periods of time wage rates well above the market-clearing level.

The issue is complicated somewhat by disagreement over what constitutes a threat of violence in the case of labor disputes. Is the practice of picketing a struck plant merely the dissemination of information? Or is it a physical barrier to anyone who wants to work for the struck employer? How about *mass* picketing? Jeers and insults directed at those who cross the picket line? What is the difference between a genuine threat and a mere expression of anger?

PRINCIPALS, AGENTS, AND POWER

What are the moral obligations of union leaders? Many of those who believe that justice requires us to respect the right of workers to join unions and bargain collectively with employers also believe that justice requires union leaders to consider the common good or the public interest in setting their goals.

This belief is closely akin to the "social responsibility of business" argument often put forward by moral critics of the economic system. Under this doctrine, corporate executives are supposed to aim not at maximum net revenue for the corporation but at some broader set of objectives that incorporate the public interest or the common good. A currently popular version of this argument is the "stakeholder thesis," which asserts that the shareholders of large corporations are merely one group of stakeholders in the corporation. Other stakeholders include the corporations' employees, suppliers, and customers as well as the communities in which they are located.

Most presentations of the stakeholder thesis confuse the issue by arguing that net revenues will actually be larger if corporate managers do care for the interests of all stakeholders. If this were true, there would be no conflict between the shareholder thesis and the stakeholder thesis. In one sense it is obviously true. The managers of corporations require the goodwill and cooperation of employees, suppliers, and customers, and so will have incentives to pay attention to the interests of these groups in order to maximize the returns to shareholders. Advocates of the stakeholder thesis must want more than this if they are saying anything relevant. So let us assume that they are assigning managers the duty of trading off some amount of shareholder income in order to pay just attention to the interests of other supposed stakeholders.

How much should they trade off? Trivial amounts can be justified as contributions toward the creation of goodwill and thus, in the long run, in the interest of shareholders. But what should be the criteria employed by the managers of large, publicly held corporations when they decide that an enhancement of one group's well-being is worth the reduction of another group's well-being? Doesn't the stakeholder thesis implicitly elevate corporate managers into benevolent despots?

Similar questions must be directed at those who want union leaders to set their goals in terms of something broader and grander than the interests of union members. Union leaders are the agents of the members just as corporate executives are the agents of the shareholders. Union leaders have fiduciary obligations that should prohibit them from sacrificing the interests of their members to their own notions of the greater public good. If either union leaders or corporate executives have the power to act contrary to the interests of their principals, their power ought to be constrained. That is a moral argument. The economic or political argument asserts that their power will be constrained, or taken away, if they begin to behave in the manner that advocates of the social responsibility doctrine want them to behave.

None of this is intended to assert that agents should be unscrupulous or ruthless. They ought to conform their behavior not only to the law but also to the accepted conventions and moral principles applicable to their profession. Agents who go beyond these boundaries will not ordinarily be working in the long-run interest of their principals. But within these boundaries, they should be permitted to make their decisions according to what they believe will most effectively advance the interests of those whom they are paid to represent. Labor union leaders are not employed by the government or the nation at large. Moral condemnations based on the mere fact that they are not acting in the public interest are completely misguided.

INDIVIDUALISM AND LABOR UNIONS

The carpenters union in the United States is officially known as the Brotherhood of Carpenters. Whatever the actual level of fraternal feeling is among union members today, there was a time when labor unions did have a great deal in common with such organizations as the Fraternal Order of Eagles and the Benevolent and Protective Order of Elks. Ought we to wish for those days to return?

Markets exercise a powerful centrifugal force in modern society. Adam Smith observed that in "civilized society" each person "stands at all times in need of the cooperation and assistance of great multitudes, while his whole life is scarce sufficient to gain the friendship of a few persons."[7] That presents an interesting dilemma. We cannot begin to produce on our own even the goods we need for survival, much less the goods that create our ordinary comforts. And we don't have enough time in our whole lives to find and make friends of people who would be able to help us produce what we want. Yet we do survive, and survive very well indeed. How do we do it?

7. Adam Smith, *An Inquiry into the Nature and Causes of the Wealth of Nations*, bk. I, chap. II (Indianapolis, Ind.: Liberty Classics, 1981). Originally published in 1776.

Through the marketplace, of course. We earn money at some specialized task and use that money to register our many wants in a way that generates prices that function as information and incentives to people capable of satisfying our wants. The degree of interdependence in a modern economy is astounding, and the smoothness of its coordination is almost miraculous. We obtain "the cooperation and assistance of great multitudes," and we do it easily and quickly, because doing so does not require us to "gain the friendship" of anyone.

That is a mixed blessing. It is possible for all of us to live well, relying on "the cooperation and assistance of great multitudes," without being personally acquainted with any single person in those multitudes. That enables us to be extraordinarily independent despite the extreme degree of our mutual interdependence. We need others, but not any specific others. We therefore don't have to form friendships except with people we like, people like us. We can effectively ignore everyone else. We don't have to get involved in community activities. We don't have to learn the names of our neighbors. If we don't like the neighborhood, we can move, with the eager assistance of the real estate market and its pseudo-friendly personnel. We can live anonymously in a densely populated city.

Adam Smith worried that those who come to live in a great city will find their conduct "observed and attended to by nobody" and will therefore begin to neglect it themselves, with the result that they will abandon themselves "to every sort of low profligacy and vice." But he noted that those who join a small religious sect will emerge from their obscurity, will attract the attention of respectable society, and will thereby develop "regular and orderly" morals.[8] We seem to have lost sight of the civilizing effect of being "observed and attended to" and are extremely quick to abandon any association that starts to monitor our conduct.

8. Ibid., bk. V, chap. I, pt. III, art. III, §12.

Has a growing sense of individualism, fostered by the wealth with independence that the market provides us, contributed to the declining interest of American workers in labor unions? Has union membership shrunk so dramatically in recent decades because more and more Americans want to make it on their own? It would be absurd to suggest that a revival of unionism might counter the emphasis on personal rights to the neglect of personal obligations and the indifference toward community that have bothered a growing number of social commentators in recent years. But raising the issue enables us at least to think about a socializing function that labor unions might perform, or might once have performed, for their members.

IN CONCLUSION

This chapter began with the claim of the Roman Catholic bishops that the right of workers to organize and join labor unions ought to be respected. We might conclude by citing the opinion of Abraham Kuyper, a distinguished and influential Protestant theologian, who believed that unions advanced the cause of justice and that governments should therefore promote unions.[9] Numerous additional examples of similar views could readily be provided. Not only church commissions and ecclesiastical officials but also many others who believe themselves to be representing the common good assume, without argument, that to support labor unions is to promote justice and morality.

In June 1999, delegates to the annual convention of the American Medical Association meeting in Chicago voted to organize a labor union for physicians, specifically for salaried physicians and medical

9. Kuyper's social theory is explained and defended by John P. Tiemstra, "Every Square Inch: Kuyperian Social Theory and Economics," in *Religion and Economics: Normative Social Theory*, ed. James M. Dean and A.M.C. Waterman (Boston, Mass.: Kluwer Academic Publishers, 1999), pp. 85–98.

residents, which together represent about a third of the nation's 620,000 practicing physicians. The AMA also announced its intention to work toward unionization of the 325,000 self-employed doctors in the United States. That will require some legislative assistance. Because self-employed doctors are clearly not employees, any attempts on their part to raise their incomes through concerted action will run afoul of the Sherman Act and its prohibitions of contracts, combinations, or conspiracies in restraint of trade. The chairman of the AMA board of trustees stated that the objective of unionization on the part of physicians would be to make sure that patient care is not sacrificed for the sake of profits.[10]

The only conclusion to be drawn at the end will be brief. We should not assume without reflection and examination of the case at issue that to support labor unions is to promote justice and morality.

10. Information on the AMA convention was taken from a syndicated *New York Times* article of June 24, 1999.

INDEX